Through Hubbel's use of stories and insightful questions, she shows us how to assess our internal dialogue and to clearly see its impact—for good or bad—on our lives and on all our relationships. Hubbel then provides practical tools to tame and improve our internal talk so we can become greater influences for good and prosperity in all our relationships. As leaders, it's important to periodically pause and remember the power of our words to influence the teams we lead. Hubbel's **WordFood** diet can certainly help us "stay on track" to becoming or remaining the type of leader people want to follow—those who are hopeful, inspiring and encouraging.

—Sidney Johnson, Vice President,
Global Supply Management

Words can be a lot like mushrooms; some are tasty, some toxic, some downright deadly. Have you ever hung out with someone who makes you strong and helps you grow? Or perhaps you've been in a toxic relationship with a person whose very presence makes you sick. You've no doubt seen words that are spoken in anger kill a friendship. If so, then you've experienced the power of **WordFood**. Everything you say either feeds, starves or poisons those around you. Even those private, internal conversations, the little things you say to yourself every day, can energize—or debilitate.

This book is a journey. Like a visitor sampling the cuisine of a foreign country, some items will be familiar and some totally new. You'll learn to look at language in a whole new way, and begin to listen to every conversation with a deeper understanding. You'll learn how to encourage and empower others, and how to protect yourself from unhealthy excess. You'll learn how to ask for the verbal nutrition you need, and how to nourish all of the relationships in your life.

This book has the power to transform your friends, your family, your work, your world, just by mobilizing the nutritional power of words.

—Orvel Ray Wilson, CSP

The concept of **WordFood** is both fundamental and transformative. It seems so easy to appreciate the power of positive thinking, but so common to avoid doing it in practice. The self-reflection and proactive techniques outlined here are very actionable and can serve as a helpful reminder or a new beginning for anyone reading this book!

—Brad D. Smith, President and CEO, Intuit

The philosopher Ernest Holmes once said, "Wouldn't it be wonderful, indeed, if everyone were for something and against nothing?" That's how I viewed this book. Wouldn't it be wonderful, indeed, if we realized that words matter and that we can have a positive impact on ourselves, our communities and the world by following the guidelines in **WordFood**? Imagine an increase in personal responsibility, civility and harmony. From individuals to communities to nations, maybe we can talk our way out of conflict and into peace. Wonderful, indeed.

—Carol A. Haave, former Deputy Under Secretary of Defense for Counterintelligence and Security

WORDFOOD

How We Feed Or Starve Our Relationships

JULIA HUBBEL

WORDFOOD™

Edited by Barbara Munson, Munson Communications

Cover design and interior page layout by Kerrie Lian,
under contract with MacGraphics Services: www.MacGraphics.net

Printed in the United States of America.

First edition

ISBN: 978-0-9828631-0-7

Library of Congress Control Number: 2010913075

The Hubbel Group, Inc.
P. O. Box 27352
Lakewood, CO 80227
720-221-7335

This book is dedicated to Rich. Thanks for being who you are.

To Orvel Ray, whose guidance in all things personal and professional has been WordFood of the first order, and whose friendship I treasure.

Acknowledgments

It takes a community to create a book, and this book owes its existence to many talented and generous people. First and foremost to my parents, who imbued in me the passion for words. To my beloved book coach, Orvel Ray Wilson, whose undying enthusiasm for this project kept me focused and dedicated, thank you. Your incredible skill, insight, love for words, ideas and brilliant coaching brought this project from inception to reality in just a few amazing months. You walk on water. When you look in the mirror I hope you see what I see—the best there is. To Ted Simmons for his skilled artistry, many great suggestions, moral support and competent eye, but above all for his forever friendship. To Grace Tiscareño-Sato, Karen Wright and Janelle Barlow for their brilliant commentary on the book. Barb Munson, whose talented editing and word wizardry makes any project shine, you're a blessing. Karen Reddick for her fine proofreading and last minute detail work, thank you. And to Kerrie Lian, whose gifted eye created my cover and interior design, many kudos. To my family members, friends and fellow travelers who provided me the stories this book contains, my heartfelt thanks to you for sharing your lives with me so that we could change the lives of others. To all who had a comment, suggestion, idea—and there were many of you, too many to name here, you know who you are—thank you from the bottom of my heart. Your contributions made all the difference.

Contents

Introduction xiii

Chapter One   Words 1

Chapter Two   How Healthy Is Your WordFood Diet?........... 5

Chapter Three   WordFood Relationships.............................. 11

Chapter Four   The WordFood Pyramid.............................. 17

                                   HeartBreads............................. 19
                                   Energy Enhancers 21
                                   Character Fiber......................... 22
                                   Balance Builders 23

Chapter Five   The WordFood Diets.................................... 29

                                   Starvation 31
                                   Bread & Water.......................... 41
                                   Ballpark 52
                                   Meat & Potatoes....................... 66
                                   Ice Cream & Cake..................... 78
                                   Devil's Food............................. 91
                                   Balanced................................. 102

Chapter Six   WordFood Spices and JunkFood 119

Chapter Seven   WordFood Poisoning 131

Chapter Eight   WordFood and Technology....................... 143

Chapter Nine   WordFood Across Generations................... 151

Chapter Ten   Wrapping It Up 159

Chapter Eleven   Authentic Conversations........................... 165

WordFood Extra: "The Rule" 209

Introduction

"You fat, ugly pig!"

It was a warm January morning in Melbourne in 1987. I stood before the bathroom mirror, taking in my 205 pounds and 52-inch hips.

You see, I had bought into the myth that a woman is just *supposed* to get fat after 30. I was tired, flabby and working as a motivational speaker.

The indignation struck like a lightning bolt. "*How dare you,*" said the voice in my head. "How *dare* you put yourself out to the community as an expert when you can't even control your own eating habits? How dare you *just give up when you're only 31?*"

Charlie, my next-door neighbor, was an *Aukker* (Australian for "redneck") and a triathlete. From his porch he'd watch me lumber down the street as I struggled to jog three miles a day. The problem wasn't that I didn't exercise; my problem was that I ate badly.

Every Friday morning he'd come 'round pounding on my door and yell, "Oy! Ya bloody Yankee sheila! Come on out and run!"

Out of a mixture of fear and embarrassment, I had always declined. Today was different. He picked up the rusty red 10-speed that had been sitting on my porch for months.

"Oy!" he yelled again. "Ya wan' me to teach ya howta roide this boike?"

Twenty-four miles later I was hooked. Then Charlie went through my cupboards and we threw out the junk food. That morning was a turning point in my life. Within a month I had lost forty pounds. By the end of the year I had lost eighty pounds.

What changed? Charlie taught me that not only was I feeding myself toxic food, I was also feeding myself toxic *words*.

When I first heard that, I was dumbfounded. Toxic words? What was Charlie talking about? Then I sat down and thought about it—and the light bulb went on. I was feeding myself words that were hurting me. I was telling myself negative things and believing them. Yes, toxic words all right. Charlie's lessons changed everything.

CHAPTER ONE

Words

The thought manifests as the word;

The word manifests as the deed;

The deed develops into habits;

And habit hardens into character

So watch the thought and its ways with care,

And let it spring from love

Born out of concern for all beings.

—Attributed to the Buddha

With a word, you can cut a coworker right to the bone or lift your spouse to the stars. Words of love can take us to the moon. The wrong words can bring us crashing back to the earth. Words can be felt as bullets, bombs or bayonets. They can be experienced as soothing blankets or energizing jolts of motivation.

Words have the power to transform. They can change the course of a life, alter our perspective, make us happy or sad. They can tear us apart or make us whole. When we direct them at ourselves, they can build us up or tear us down. They help us see problems from a new perspective, and help lift us out of the doldrums.

The thing about words is that they are interpreted differently by all of the people in our lives. And, more often than not, the impact our words have on others is unintentional. We are oblivious to their power. We are swept along by our emotions and we let our words come tumbling out unfettered.

Words have both a terrible and a wonderful power: to heal, to hurt, to help, to grace or disgrace. With this power comes the responsibility to wield our words wisely. Our ability to uplift each other with words is a true gift, while the capacity to do damage—even when we do so without thinking—is a curse. And, with our busy lives and the pervasive use of instant online communications these days, it's more challenging than ever to remain aware of the words we're using and their impact on others.

WELCOME TO WORDFOOD

Simply put, WordFood is what we say to one another, the words that we speak. It is how we feed or starve our relationships…how we grace or disgrace each other with our language.

Words are to the mind what food is to the body. We take them in as mental and emotional nourishment. When we speak to someone, or even to ourselves, the words we serve up, together with our tone and posture, form a kind of psychological "meal." Just like physical food, our messages can be digested and absorbed by our mental and emotional bodies. The verbal meal we provide can be nourishing or it can be toxic.

This is *WordFood*, the diet of messages we feed ourselves and others every day, from the moment we get up in the morning and begin those mental conversations with ourselves, to the exchanges we have with our spouses, our children, our working peers, our employees, clients, customers and strangers. These conversations continue all day long and they have a tremendous impact on our psychological and emotional lives and the lives of others.

We get our diet of WordFood from the words we take in. We also get it from various impressions, including the advertising that we see, the television shows we watch, the radio stations we tune in to and the music we enjoy. Our WordFood "Diet" extends to the causes and communities that we get involved with, from Save the Whales to the Tea Party Movement to the political party of our choice. The messages we feed ourselves, through the media and the mentality of our friends, mix with our own internal dialogue and become our daily bread of thoughts, ideas and feelings.

When your WordFood Diet is healthy, the inevitable ups and downs of the day are much easier to bear. You feel stronger and more resilient, mentally and emotionally. And when you use words to grace others you are doing the same for yourself. An unhealthy WordFood Diet, on the other hand, can lead to all sorts of disharmony, as we shall see.

THE REASON FOR THIS BOOK

The first purpose of this book is to feed you. Your relationship with yourself is the most important one you will ever have. No one deserves your love and positive regard more than you. This book is all about how you feed or starve your relationships, and that begins with yourself. It will teach you how to feed yourself a healthy diet of WordFood so you can live a rich, vibrant life and also give the world your very best.

The second purpose is to show you how to feed others. It will help you become more aware of what you say, how you say it and why you say it. You will hear how potent your words are, recognize the impact your words have on your relationships and discover the good you can do with a single, simple phrase. You will become more aware of how much damage a careless word can do.

In her book, *Fierce Conversations*, Susan Scott writes, "We must recognize that humans share a universal longing to be known, and being known, to be loved." True, but it is our *words*, and how we deliver them, that are responsible for conveying essential emotions like love. Our verbal nutrition tells others how we feel, and how we value another's company. Our words, body language and tone are the art forms by which we build the network of relationships in our world and express all the emotions that we feel. And when we don't feel loved, we stop expressing love to others.

But it is through the expression of positive WordFood that we engender warm feelings, and by doing so, manifest them within ourselves in return. It creates reciprocity. What we give, we get back. Moreover, by being willing to use the power of our words to express love, regard and respect to others first, we open the channel by which it is likely to come back to us in return. We must be willing to start the communication by feeding others powerful, positive WordFood.

On a grander scale, imagine a world where people don't fear each other's words. This can happen! By our choice of WordFood we can little by little change the world. The result can be a world of greater connectedness and warmth. This book can help bring about that change.

CHAPTER TWO

How Healthy Is Your WordFood Diet?

Do you realize that when you wake up in the morning and say something angry or abusive to yourself, you set the tone for the entire day? How many times has that early-morning voice inside your head said something like:

> *"I'm such an idiot."*
>
> *"Guess I'm just getting older."*
>
> *"These gawd-damn pants must have shrunk in the dryer."*
>
> *"These kids just don't appreciate how much I do for them!"*
>
> *"I'll never be (skinny, rich, attractive, smart) enough."*
>
> *"You fat, ugly pig."*

And this spills over to those you love...

> *"If you don't hurry you'll miss the school bus!"*
>
> *"Hey! Pick up your damn (shoes, book, cereal bowl) and put it away!"*

"My (husband, wife, child) is just so (thoughtless, selfish, stupid)!"

This diet of toxic words then cascades downward. That ugly tone touches the people you love at the breakfast table, and then spills over onto the people at work and throughout the rest of the day. The cruelty you show to yourself is both destructive and contagious.

Alternatively, supportive and caring words spoken to yourself upon arising have the power to touch your heart and soul with grace and carry you throughout the day, leaving others graced and uplifted. Have you ever started your day by saying one of the following?

"Good morning, gorgeous!"

"I love you!"

"I'm so proud of you."

"You're so (pretty, sexy, handsome) in this light."

"Go get 'em, big guy."

"That outfit looks great on you."

"You're going to make a difference today!"

When you pay attention to how your words affect yourself and others, you will see their power. Others feel energized by your positive expectations and want to be in your presence. Your words leave them feeling better about themselves and about the possibilities in life. They also appreciate who you are and the energy you bring to situations.

Your WordFood can be eloquent. Throughout the ages, others have inspired us with their words—perhaps a great president, a poet or an orator. And we are touched by the words of journalists, novelists and playwrights.

I bet you can remember who said:

> *"I have a dream…"*
>
> *"Ask not what your country can do for you…"*
>
> *"That's one small step for Man…"*
>
> *"Read my lips. No new taxes!"*
>
> *"The needs of the many outweigh the needs of the few, or the one."*

These phrases are burned into our hearts, minds and souls. They have moved us to tears, to anger, to laughter, to action. They have inspired us to rise above our fears, to go beyond what we thought we could do and achieve much more.

Or your WordFood can be simple. "Mmmm, doughnuts!" comes to mind. Most of us aren't eloquent speakers, but that doesn't mean we're not being listened to. Even if you're not very expressive by nature or are a quiet person, never assume that you aren't impacting those around you. Even if you have never taken a communication class in college, or attended college at all, know that your words are very powerful and do make a difference.

THE MAGICAL GIFT

Each of us has this gift, this ability to touch another human heart with words. But make no mistake, no one but you is responsible for what you say, the intentions behind your words and the impact they have. Consider this: How magical would it be to be able to move people to greatness, to have a powerful, positive effect on others? You can! It starts with having that effect on yourself, on your own soul, each and every day, when you look at yourself in the mirror and feed yourself those first words of the day.

What is the WordFood meal that you are feeding yourself? What kind of verbal nutrition are you giving your soul so that you can then feed others? How are you affecting your spouse, your friends, your peers, your employees and community members? Are you giving them what they need to thrive? What about your children? We use language to teach our children how to make their way in the world. They learn about their own value through our feedback, our word pictures of them.

HOW WORDFOOD WORKS

Given that our language is versatile and varied, you're going to find that you use a broad range of WordFood with different people in different situations. The dynamics of that relationship, your mood, and your level of trust or fear will come into play. During the course of any day, at home or at work, you'll be faced with people, in differing moods, who want different things from you, who place different demands on you. Each of these situations may require a different WordFood response.

Have you ever noticed how your conversations shift with the mood? Have you seen how you can suddenly find yourself caught up in an argument, deadlocked in angry silence, decide to make up, and then find yourself relaxed and happy again? Sure you do. And in that way, you find yourself engaging in many different "diets" with others over the course of a day, an hour, or even a few minutes.

Emotions often drive our choice of words, and as a result we find our language changing with our moods. With happiness or anger, pain or pleasure, joy or heartbreak, our words and tone mirror our feelings. We may feel disapproval and voice it, leaving a dent in someone's self-esteem. We may express deep affection that warms a friend's heart. Either way, our words have impact, and as others choose to hear those words, how they filter them into their being is critical to their health. Just as important, how we hear words and filter them is critical to our own well being. Our words can also drive our emotions.

THE WORDFOOD DIETS

Each person affects you differently and will get a different response from you at different times depending on your mood, the events of the day, the weather, or any number of factors. You may think you're behaving the same with everyone, but you most likely are not. Each of us is touched uniquely by different relationships, and they draw varying reactions and, as a result, responses from different WordFood Diets. We like to think that we're consistent, but life demands much more of us.

Consider stress. The greater the stress, the more exaggerated the symptoms and negativity will be, and this is when the less healthy WordFood Diets come into play. When you are feeling unhappy, under pressure, hurt, criticized, inadequate or in some other awkward state, you're already likely to be expressing words from one of the dysfunctional WordFood Diets. When the stress increases, your reactions are likely to escalate in response. Your words become more hurtful and damaging as you try to protect yourself, and you end up creating greater havoc.

But the stress you feel can be helped by an internal conversation from a healthy WordFood Diet. Speak to yourself with care and appreciation, even in times of great stress. That inner dialogue can be very calming, causing that potential escalation to slow down, or even stop.

"I can handle this."

"It's not really that bad."

"I'm in control here."

"This situation is the result of choices I've made up to now. Now I can make better choices."

"Taking complete responsibility for this gives me the ability to respond in a more appropriate way."

Even in difficult situations you can learn to intervene by sending messages to the emotional center that's in trouble. The more your internal conversations are carried on with respect for your own psyche, the more you can extend that same regard to others.

Every conversation is an opportunity to help. Each time you speak, you have the chance to uplift someone, to leave them feeling graced. This is the power we have when we wield our language well. When you develop a healthy WordFood diet and use it every day, you will have the ability to transform the world around you.

CHAPTER THREE

WordFood Relationships

In your day-to-day life, you likely will have WordFood relationships in four different areas: your self, your work, your personal side and your community. With each relationship, you probably will use different WordFood. This may seem obvious. You would say, "I love you" to a spouse but not to a boss, and you would pray to a deity but not to a friend. WordFood is about the deeper levels on which you communicate with others and the impact you have with your words. Let's look at these four WordFood relationships.

1. Self

Your relationship with yourself determines how you treat everyone else in your life. Whether you're single or living with family or roommates, how you speak to yourself when you face the mirror sets the tone for the day. From this everything else flows. You can critically impact the quality of someone's day, especially your family's, through WordFood. When you treat yourself with love first thing, then most likely the first thing out of your mouth to your family will also be love, and it will come easily and naturally. That's why it's so important that you treat yourself with respect and kindness.

"Wow, you look great."

"I'm really looking forward to today."

"This color looks really good on me."

"This shirt brings out the color of my eyes."

"I have important work to do today, and I'm grateful for it."

See yourself for the first time. Appreciate the being that you are. See yourself as full of potential, able to make good choices, live well, do good in the world, and make others happy. And you can, and will, when you feed yourself well nourishing WordFood first. That ability to see yourself for the first time every day gives you permission to start every day as though it's a new beginning. The more quickly we can let go of the mistakes we've made, and forgive ourselves for our real or imagined wrongs, the more quickly we can begin to make the difference we came here for, and touch lives in the most positive way possible.

2. Work

As soon as you walk through the door at work you are met with greetings. There is work to do, deadlines to meet and people who need you. There are demands and frustrations, expressed or not. At work you may be engaged in a plethora of relationships depending on whether you're an entrepreneur, an employee, a manager or senior executive. Your perceived level of control over your own life will give you a sense of security and comfort. You may feel unhappy or threatened, or at ease and in control. You may feel overwhelmed and stressed. No matter what your work situation, your WordFood Diet will reflect your mood and feelings about those at work and the stress levels you're experiencing, as well as the level of trust you feel. When you bring an open heart and acceptance to your work relationships you can help reduce other's stress. This allows them to relax around you and feel at ease in your presence. They enjoy being around you; they look to you as a "port in the storm."

3. Personal Relationships

You may have a wide range of personal relationships depending on how engaged you are in life. Your family, friends, close relationships, your children, all make up these spheres of your world, and they all require your attention and emotional equity. Your Word-Food Diets may vary greatly among these relationships depending on the demands that these closer connections place on you, and the trust levels and commitments that you have with them. These are our most intimate involvements, our most emotional connections, and therefore some of the most stressful. Your WordFood diets will reflect both the highest joys and deepest hurts that our vulnerability to these relationships entails. Robert White, author of *Living an Extraordinary Life*, reminds us of a comment by Carl Jung that it is in relationships where the "clearest mirror" exists to tell us what we need to work on next.

4. Community

Your world may also involve community commitments such as church, shelters, charities, service clubs or other groups that gather to give back. These provide you a chance to get involved. These organizations demand your time, your energy and your emotional involvement. Your WordFood diets here will reflect how much joy you have in giving back, how much pleasure you take in participating and how much you enjoy the relationships you've developed in this environment.

Community also includes your relationship with your Master Architect, your higher power. What is that like? Is it a caring, trusting one? Do you enjoy your communications with your higher power? Do you check in regularly? Do you feel loved? Much of this is going to depend on your belief system. However, in most cases, there is a loving Source, and that Source offers complete acceptance of our humanness and, when we take responsibility, offers a willingness to forgive us for whatever we do and start over with a humble heart. Each day begins afresh without guilt, and whatever your source of divinely inspired WordFood, it will provide important guidance on your journey.

Part of the WordFood you take in consists of books, tapes and programs that you use to develop yourself spiritually. Mornings are a perfect time to find inspiration from a book of affirmations, sayings, scripture or other writings that feed you messages about your value. What better way to begin the day than with Word-Food from a holy source about love, acceptance or forgiveness? This may well be the best way to see yourself as the precious human being that you are.

A CHALLENGE

There is an implicit challenge in this book. As you read over these various WordFood Diets (beginning on page 29) and consider the model for the ideal WordFood that you will offer your four Word-Food relationships, consider who *you* are. Within each of us is a community of components: that aspect of us that does our work, the part of us that is a spouse and/or parent, the part of us that is a friend, the piece of us that goes to places of worship. These constituents sometimes speak for us, and as a wise friend of mine puts it, "write the checks in our name." Some are more functional than others. You know they are out there because every so often one of those parts speaks up, and you wonder who in the world just got you in trouble. Or you wonder what piece of you volunteered to sit on that committee. These parts can be very strong, bullheaded and sometimes not very healthy. They can be egotistical and unpredictable, as well. There are elements in us that tend to overreact when someone is unkind. There are those components of us that get very hurt and lose perspective when a loved one lashes out. And when we are feeling strong, there are parts of us that can have otherworldly courage in the face of great personal challenges. These are all facets of who we are.

This book raises the question of what part of you needs to "sit down" so that it can learn? Which constituent in you needs to get out of the way so that you can grow? Is there an aspect of you that is egotistical or fearful and keeping you from another way of seeing? Every so often this book will offer a suggestion that you may find difficult to accept, or perhaps even offensive. *These* are the suggestions that you might take an extra moment to consider because your different constituents are rising to the occasion. Something important is happening here and it's time for you to take note of your reaction. Which part is about to write off this idea before you—the real you—get a chance to consider how you might gain from the experience being suggested?

At the beginning of 2010 I decided that I wanted to get in top shape. Having been a bodybuilder for nearly thirty years and having accumulated a lot of knowledge about nutrition, I felt I had a pretty good base of knowledge by which to judge the skills of someone I might hire to be a personal trainer. After all, I had worked with personal trainers before, and this time was no different.

But was it? Here I was at 57, my body was changing, and even though I was strong and reasonably fit, I should no longer be lifting very heavy weights. My goals were different. So I asked myself what component of me needed to sit down so that I could learn, and I realized that I was basing my next choice of a personal trainer on thirty years of what was probably outdated information. I went straight to my gym and selected the most recently certified graduate from a strength and training program that I could find.

Ben, all of 24, turned out to be the best choice I could have made. His lively, challenging, whole-body programs are used by Olympic athletes and are the most up-to-the-minute in sports medicine. After being bored for the past five years, I am now inspired, delighted and pushed by the variety of his workouts because they're never the same. And I'm in the best shape of my life. By sitting that arrogant, know-it-all aspect of me down, I gained something valuable.

What part of you needs to sit down so that you can gain something here?

CHAPTER FOUR

The WordFood Pyramid

First there was the American Food Guide Pyramid, adapted by the USDA in the 1990s to help people understand and obtain better nutrition. Now there's the WordFood Pyramid, consisting of four essential WordFood groups. These dynamic building blocks represent what people need every day to thrive and succeed.

HeartBreads, the base of the Pyramid, represents the words we must hear everyday to thrive. **Energy Enhancers**, the next level, are words applied to specific actions, skills or behaviors. **Character Fiber**, the third level, is critical to personal, spiritual and professional development. **Balance Builders** are used sparingly, keep us on course. Each WordFood group has its own place in our everyday diet, for our own development and for those around us.

As you read the descriptions of each WordFood group, consider whether you're being adequately fed enough of these words every day.

Ask yourself:

> *What's missing?*
>
> *How can I get more?*
>
> *Who should be providing it to me?*
>
> *Who can I go to for better verbal nutrition?*
>
> *Who needs better verbal nutrition from me?*
>
> *Are the people around me getting too much or too little of any one WordFood group?*

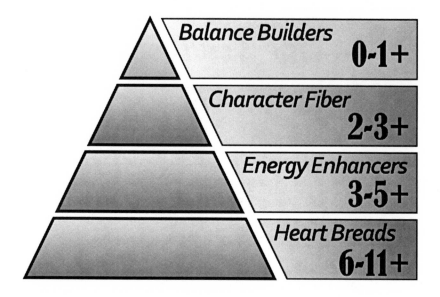

Each of these four WordFood groups is important to healthy relationships. First, you must ensure that you're cared for and well fed. Only then can you care for others in your spheres of influence at home, at work and in your community. Are you providing yourself a healthy diet of each of these groups? If the dinner table is a solemn place each night, with little conversation, perhaps your family also isn't getting enough WordFood nutrition. If your team members or employees aren't performing up to par, perhaps you aren't feeding them a nutritious diet from these key WordFood groups.

Let's take a look at these four groups and what they do.

HEARTBREADS, 6-11 SERVINGS DAILY

HeartBreads touch the human soul and inspire the heart. This group forms the backbone, the building blocks of the Word-Food Diet. These are the words that we must hear every day to thrive. These include words of praise, positive reinforcement, caring, acts of active listening, graciousness, empathy, understanding, specific feedback tied to positive behaviors, catching people in the act of doing something well, gratitude, eye contact, warmth, openness, accessibility, trust, collaboration, cooperation and open give and take.

These words support the human experience, inviting the person to live fully, to reach inside and come from trust instead of fear, to try new things. HeartBreads develop the fundamentals that establish human connections, create trust and allow relationships to evolve. Heartbreads, provided every day, support teamwork, achievement and high performance. When you use these words with yourself and others, they engender a wholly different level of functioning: *thrival* instead of survival, joy instead of woe.

HeartBreads support achievement, move people through the daily challenges and doldrums and support us through the inevitable injuries. They provide a place to be heard, a safe space to know ourselves. Generous servings of this group can stop an argument, soothe a hurt, put anger in perspective or inspire someone to greatness. This fundamental WordFood group forms the foundation of all the others. When provided every day in multiple servings, they are the main course of a healthy Word-Food Diet.

Everyday examples of HeartBreads could be:

> *"Thank you!"*

> *"I appreciate you."*

> *"Thanks for coming in so early today."*

> *"You make such a difference in my life."*

> *"Thank you for everything you do around here."*

> *"I'm sorry you feel bad. What can I do for you?"*

> *"You have a right to your opinion. I respect your viewpoint."*

> *"Thanks for taking the time to be with me today."*

> *"Your work is so valuable around here."*

> *"Thanks for your input on my project. It really helped me along."*

> *"Your smile just makes my day every morning."*

> *"You're such a fantastic husband. Thanks for loving me."*

> *"You are the best friend anyone could ever have."*

> *"I look forward to working with you every day."*

> *"I noticed your extra time in the office last week. Thank you."*

ENERGY ENHANCERS, 3-5 SERVINGS DAILY

While HeartBreads swell the heart and appeal to the emotions, Energy Enhancers swell the head and apply to a specific action, skill or behavior. The group includes compliments, acknowledgment and recognition. Energy Enhancers are all about support, providing ways to add value to someone through words of encouragement, words that build self-assurance. Regular servings feed the listener huge confidence builders about their abilities, skills or a job well done. Energy Enhancers can also provide helpful guidance on a project or assignment. People who get words from this group are thoroughly energized and pumped up. These are the compliments that raise our spirits and motivation to do much more. People walk away ready to do their best, whether it's an adult taking on a big project at work or a teen who is tackling trigonometry.

Examples of Energy Enhancers:

"You look great in that dress!"

"That was a super job you did on the Aspen Project."

"You have excellent instincts for customer relations."

"You are the best cook in the southwest!"

"I wish I could ski like you do. Would you coach me?"

"You are beautiful."

"That was masterful work on your presentation."

"You've come a long way on your math skills. I'm so proud of you."

"I admire your ability to research in such detail."

"You made all the difference on the conference planning team."

"Your enthusiasm lifts everyone's spirits in this office."

"Your leadership skills have impressed me very much."

"You are so handsome in that suit. I'm proud to be seen with you."

CHARACTER FIBER, 2-3 SERVINGS DAILY

The WordFood Character Fiber words are all about developing power and depth, providing course correction, setting boundaries and guidelines. This WordFood group creates better "bodies" through clarity and honesty, through giving guidance about life direction. It is used during coaching and counseling, through mentoring and management, where a strong and caring hand is necessary to help provide perspective and judgment in challenging situations. When life offers opportunities through challenges, it's time to seek guidance, and Character Fiber is the source. There is also an internal "voice" that speaks to us. Sources for this voice are found in spiritual authorities, universities, senior management and friends. Servings of Character Fiber are critical to personal, spiritual and professional development and, while it's sometimes taxing, it's always ultimately rewarding to live up to an opportunity for growth. This WordFood group also sets safe boundaries for how we wish to be treated by others.

Examples of Character Fiber:

> *"My observation of your interactive skills is that they could use some work. Let's talk about this some more. I know you've got the ability to be more effective in this area."*

> *"You're very good with your individual relationships on your team but your strategic vision can sometimes be lacking. Let's set a time when we can go over your long-term goals and develop a vision for your department. I want you to achieve a promotion in the next few years and this is a key part of your development."*

> *"You've set some challenging goals for yourself but you've excluded your family and friends from helping you achieve them. Perhaps it's time for you to stop being a loner and start receiving their love and support. It's hard enough to set yourself lofty aspirations, but to isolate yourself is even harder. Let's talk about how to learn to receive the love that your family and friends want to give you to help you reach your goals, so that they can be there for you when you make it to the top."*

BALANCE BUILDERS, USE SPARINGLY

Balance Builders, at the top of the Pyramid, keep the pendulum from swinging too far in either direction. They keep us on course. Used sparingly, these words are appropriate when someone is absolutely misbehaving or about to go off the deep end. Words in this group may also be for those who are reaching life's heights. Effective living requires balance, and this WordFood group addresses behaviors that are either in the high achievement category, which comes with top awards and acknowledgment, or are destructive behaviors that threaten to undermine.

Words of critique are sometimes important to show that there are areas needing improvement or when someone is not living up to expectations, standards or agreements. They also are used when someone is letting others down, misbehaving or hurting others, or when we ourselves are being hurt or lied to. WordFood in this group challenges other's toxic behavior, ill treatment, the overstepping of boundaries, lack of respect and other misbehaviors, but done so in a spirit of respect and by setting an example. At the other end of the spectrum, Balance Builders pay the maximum regard to incredible performance with high praise and compliments, sweet words and accolades but come only on rare occasions when called for, keeping one's ego under control.

"It's clear that you've been experiencing stress, but your behavior has impacted other team members and this has shown up in their performance as well as your own. It's time to step down as team leader for a while and reconsider your best role in the company."

"We all look up to the example you have set for extraordinary achievement here at Ball Company. Your impressive history at the company speaks for itself. We hope that young managers continue to learn from you. Thank you for your service."

"You are disappointing yourself and me by not living up to the expectations of this position. You have the skills and the intelligence to do this job. And you came here highly recommended. For your own reasons you

*have made other choices with your time. This has
had an unfortunate effect on a number of people
who counted on you, including me. I am invested in
salvaging this situation. What are you willing to do to
help remedy it?"*

Two important questions that you could ask yourself are:

*"What would be the first indication that my
performance is improving"?*

*"If a miracle solved my performance problem, what
would I be doing differently tomorrow?"*

—Heath & Heath, *Switch: How to Change Things When Change Is
Hard*, Crown Business, 2010

Each of the WordFood groups offers key verbal nutrition when
taken in their appropriate daily amounts. But any of them, offered
in excess, can affect both the giver and receiver. Everyone needs
a certain amount of Character Fiber during the day, and there is
occasionally a call for Balance Builders when there is a problem
with performance. By any measure, the majority of your daily
interactions call for HeartBreads, which will work to enhance
those interactions and prevent most communication problems
from developing in the first place. You'll find that there are some
people in your life who need more of certain WordFood groups
than others. You simply adjust.

Keep in mind that relationships don't thrive without feedback. People can hurt us, and we need to establish and defend our boundaries. This also is the role of Balance Builders. But sometimes you
have to be more forceful if you are being hurt.

There is a story about the Buddha, who was traveling through
India. He had finished his teaching in a particular village and was

ready to leave. One of the elders asked which way he was planning to go and the Buddha pointed west.

The man said, "Holy Buddha, you don't want to go in that direction. You want to go in this direction," and he pointed east. The Buddha asked, "Why?"

The man said, "To the west is a terrible snake that is biting all the people. It is not safe."

The Buddha said, "I will go west." And off he strode.

As the Buddha walked west, he watched for the snake. Sure enough, not far outside the village, the snake revealed itself.

"Great Buddha," the snake said, "I recognize you. I will not bite you. You may pass."

The Buddha looked the snake in the eye and said, "I hear you've been misbehaving. You've been biting the villagers. Doing terrible things."

The snake hung its head.

"It's true," he said.

"This must stop at once," demanded the Buddha. "I will come by here again soon and I will check on you."

The Buddha continued on his way. A few months later he was back in the village. He heard nothing about the snake among the villagers. When he was done with his teachings, he went out to find the snake.

He searched long and hard. Finally he came upon it.

The snake was lying there, bloody and broken, beaten to a pulp.

"My goodness! What happened to you?" cried the Buddha.

"I did what you told me," said the snake. "I stopped biting the villagers. They got bold. They came out here with sticks and rocks and beat me within an inch of my life!"

"You idiot!" said the Buddha. "I told you not to bite. I didn't tell you not to hiss!"

It is important to set boundaries with our words. While we should be kind, we needn't be doormats. We have the right to stand up for ourselves, our safety and our psychological and emotional well being.

These four groups from the WordFood Pyramid each play a huge role in our interactions with others. Keep them in mind to serve up when someone's Diet calls for more. Let's look at those Diets next.

CHAPTER FIVE

The WordFood Diets

Do you ever get the impression that someone is feeding you misinformation? Or that you're being served up a plate of bulls__t? Or perhaps you're getting pablum, the kind of bland diet where you can hold a phone away from your ear for a few minutes while someone is talking, bring it back and the person still hasn't said anything of substance.

Whether it's at home or at the office, you're always being fed a diet of some kind of WordFood—positive or negative or somewhere in between. In some cases, it can be a very specific diet of words because it springs from a particular kind of intent. And many of these diets can leave you feeling distinctly uncomfortable. The person's intent can range from anger and fear to rejection and insecurity—the whole spectrum of negative human emotions.

The trick is to identify the diet that you're being fed, and to reach out and engage that person in such a way as to bring him or her back to a healthy, positive exchange.

These next pages explore seven diets—six dysfunctional, one highly functional—that you can identify, understand and respond to with servings from the WordFood Pyramid. With the right responses, patience and understanding, in many cases you can reach past what you're being fed by the person dishing out the diet, develop a new connection and change the conversation. Ultimately you will develop your skills so that your interactions create a primarily Balanced WordFood Diet, and that you are regularly drawing from each of the four groups of the WordFood Pyramid every day and in all your relationships.

Bon appétit!

STARVATION DIET

Marta is Ray's boss. She is from Columbia and has been in the United States for about twelve years. She is proud of her heritage. She is very proud of how far she has come. She likes to have her name pronounced correctly. Everyone at work, except Ray, has learned how to pronounce her name with a hard "T." Mar-*ta*.

Marta has told her Hispanic colleagues at the plant that Ray doesn't respect her authority. "That is why he won't pronounce my name correctly," she says. "He's trying to undermine my authority. He's doing this on purpose in front of the others to show them who's boss."

Ray is a thirty-five year veteran of the plant, and a bit deaf as a result of all those years working with loud machinery. He likes his boss a lot, and enjoys bringing Marta her favorite dark espresso in the morning. He tries to flirt with her because she's pretty. He's not sure why she keeps reminding him of her name—all he hears is "Martha."

When Ray comes in this morning, he opens her office door and says, "Good morning, Martha, here's your espresso!" Marta seethes and decides she's not going to talk to Ray at all. Even if she is responsible for managing him, she's had it. She'll teach him a lesson. She refuses the coffee and turns her back. She's giving Ray the WordFood equivalent of the Starvation Diet.

Characteristics

When you're being fed a Starvation Diet, you get silence, the dismissal. No matter what you do, there is no response, no interaction, no feedback. You're living in a vacuum of information, without any kind of exchange. You're left out in the cold to figure out the rules of the engagement on your own. You find yourself starving for information, any hint of emotion, a subtlety. Any crumb will do. You begin to project your own ideas and imaginings onto the relationship to create something, anything at all. In a vacuum, you often imagine the worst.

This happens when there's a real or perceived hurt, offense, insult or injustice. The other person feels injured and is punishing you through the silent treatment. You may have committed a minor slight or a major infraction. Or there may have been a long history of real or imagined wrongs that have finally led up to a decision to shut you out without telling you why, and suddenly you're locked out without an explanation.

As with Marta and Ray, there could have been a cultural misunderstanding or a misinterpreted remark. Or something private may be going on in the person's life that is too hard to discuss and they are taking it out on you. You may have committed a long series of microinequities and the last one was the last straw.

WordFood from these folks more often than not is…

…silence.

Food for Thought

"Microinequities" refers to the ways in which individuals are either "singled out, or overlooked, ignored, or otherwise discounted" based on an unchangeable characteristic such as race or gender. A microinequity generally takes the form of a gesture, different kind of language, treatment, or even tone of voice. It is suggested that the perceptions that cause the manifestation of microinequities are deeply rooted and unconscious. The cumulative effect of microinequities can impair a person's performance in the workplace or classroom, damage self-esteem, and may eventually lead to that person's withdrawal from the situation.

—Wikipedia, 2010

Whether the WordFood is spoken or silent, body language can include an expressionless face and cold eyes. Their arms are crossed and you're faced with a closed body position. Avoiding eye contact is also common. You're likely to hear flat monotone speech and a cold voice tone. They may turn their back on you or turn their body partly to the side to avoid direct face-to-face contact. They may be abrupt, rude, use few words to get across what has to be said and dismiss you right away.

For the most part, though, you are faced with avoidance behaviors. The fears behind the behavior may communicate:

> *I've been hurt, and I don't want to be hurt again.*
>
> *You're forbidden from hurting me again.*
>
> *I'm going to make you pay for what you did. I will never lose control again.*
>
> *I'm going to make you suffer.*

The motivations behind this behavior might include:

> *I don't trust you.*
>
> *I fear a loss of control.*
>
> *If you get information (or something else I value) from me, you can take my (power, authority, something else I value) away.*

Common negative responses to this WordFood Diet:

> *"He's a control freak. He can't let go of anything so he has to micromanage."*

> *"You just can't talk to her. Forget about it, leave her alone. It's a waste of time."*

> *"You can't work with these people. It's like talking to a brick wall."*

> *"That arrogant S.O.B.!"*

WHAT TO EXPECT FROM THIS WORDFOOD DIET

Behaviors that you are likely to encounter when someone is feeding you a Starvation Diet are listed below. You'll also find an appropriate response for handling that WordFood so you aren't negatively swept up and find yourself angry and frustrated and, therefore, responding in kind.

Silent Treatment: You get nothing at all. You're ignored completely. The appropriate response is to let it go. However, don't ignore it in anger. Simply accept the behavior as where this person is at the moment. Let things be as they are and wait for another time to try to talk.

Starved for Words: You get few, if any, words. The effective response is to show up on their doorstep with topics in mind to get them started talking. Pick three essential items that you know are of real importance to them: items that have deadlines, items of emotional importance, items of interest. Don't push or try to force the issue, simply suggest that you begin a conversation. Be inviting, warm and open. Be more of a supplicant. Remember that they are likely to have been feeling hurt.

Punishes Through Silence: Another version of the silent treatment; here the silence is deafening and accompanied by angry body language. The appropriate response is to say, "You're right, I'm wrong, how can we get through this?" Begin with this gentle apology. It does not matter who is right or wrong. The purpose is to start a dialogue and to establish open communication. The bigger person is going to say "I'm sorry" first and create the opening for connection. This allows the hurt person to retain her dignity and move through the anger enough to start talking, either about a neutral topic or about the issue at hand. Either way this is a healthy start toward dialogue.

One Word Answers: Every attempt you make to engage with good questions engenders nothing but terse answers. You might get anything from "No," "I doubt it" and "I'll pass" to "If you say so." The appropriate response is to prime the pump to start somewhere. Keep working the angles until you find that spot where there is a willingness to start talking, whether it's a sentence or a paragraph. What can you talk about? What constitutes safe ground? Take responsibility for the conversation and keep trying. You might try repeating their response back to them as a question.

"Is there a problem with my work?"

"No."

"No?" (Don't attempt to expand on or challenge their responses. Just wait for them to elaborate.)

"No. It's not your work that's the problem. It's …"

Don't force, be gentle, be warm, be open, and remember that most likely there are hurt feelings, and possibly a long history of hurt feelings on the other side. In some cases the silent treatment happens after someone has been hurt repeatedly over a long period and this is a wall that has been put up for that person's protection. It won't come down easily, and trust has to be won back over time. You may have to earn your way back over a wall that either you, or someone else, has caused to be built.

Talk to the Hand: You're facing the palm. You've gotten a rude gesture that indicates you're not welcome and you're intruding. However, you care about this person, and life and/or work have to go on. One way or another you have to get past this person's anger. An appropriate response might be, "I've hurt you. I'm sorry. Let's get past this. What can we do from here?" The purpose here is to offer the olive branch and try to start a conversation, to begin a healing process. Whether someone has taken offense, has built up vitriol or is just angry in the moment, your peacemaking could make all the difference. Again, it doesn't matter who is at fault.

Eats at Me: The silence is hurting you (both of you, your lives, a work project, things you care about). When the silence between you has gone on for a long time and you are both suffering in your relationship, you're being fed a Starvation Diet instead of emotional food. Your relationship can't survive on this kind of input. No matter who started it, no matter what the initiating circumstances were, it doesn't matter anymore. There is a good chance that others are paying the price for your standoff: family members, team members, friends, part of your community who are being hurt by your unwillingness to bury the hatchet.

An appropriate response could be:

> *"This situation is hurting both of us (and others as well). There is a larger issue at stake here. Let me apologize for my part of it. Let's please move beyond this and work together. Here's how I suggest that we proceed."*

In each of the suggested responses above you can see a positive communication is being applied that seeks to overcome the real or imagined pain behind the Starvation Diet behavior. These come from the WordFood Pyramid and constitute multiple servings of supportive and caring HeartBreads, where you are gently inquiring about what's been lost, the imagined injury or pain endured. You are also using Character Fiber where there are some coaching skills involved to find out what the fear is. Someone must apologize, and it doesn't matter who. The door needs to be opened to start the conversation again. HeartBreads, including courtesy, grace and tenderness, go a long way to opening the door when there are silence and fear on the other side.

BRIDGING THE GAP

Back to Ray and Marta. They both have options in dealing with each other. Ray has no idea what he's done to create the problem. Marta's pride and ego have gotten in the way. Marta could choose to quiet her pride and look to her leadership role for some Character Fiber phrases instead. She might say:

> *"Ray, I am uncomfortable in this relationship and I would like to fix that. Are you aware that it bothers me when you mispronounce my name?"*
>
> *"Ray, I may have made an assumption about you that wasn't fair. Why do you keep calling me Martha?"*
>
> *"Ray, I appreciate the espresso you bring me every morning, but I don't understand why you keep calling me Martha. Help me understand why you do this."*
>
> *"Ray, I'm very frustrated that you still do not know*

> *how to say my name. It is MAR-TA, not MAR-THA. Can you hear the difference?"*

Ray could approach Marta to find out about her silence.

> *"Martha, I am sorry I offended you. May I please find out what I did to displease you?"*
>
> *"I apologize for whatever I have done wrong. Please let me know so that I can make things right with you again."*
>
> *"I am a little hard of hearing, and so sometimes I misunderstand. I may not have heard something you said correctly. Please let me know if I misunderstood something you said."*

Marta's ego and pride are blocking the communication, and compromising her ability to manage. Other employees are watching how she's handling this situation. Either party can put an end to this. While Marta would be wise to let it go, it could be Ray's kind and humble inquiry that could force her to see how her pride is undermining her leadership.

The first intention here is to do no further damage. Approach the other person with an open heart. Be prepared for the possibility that you might be attacked, accused, belittled, dumped on or further ignored. Someone who has been bottling things up for a while could well be ready to let it all out in an explosive outburst. It's important not to take things personally and to let it all go by you, not to take it in as an insult. This could well be the key step in a healing process, which is just now beginning because you opened the door—and good for you for having the courage to do it. If you are the cause of the hurt, the hurt could well be exaggerated for dramatic effect. Don't rise to the bait or argue. It takes courage not to respond when someone is expressing anger like this, but know that it will pass. Just let things work their way through. Once this person has vented, it's possible to begin a brand new conversation at another level. When it does, it will be a great gift for you both, and everyone around you.

Starvation	Responses
Silent Treatment	Ignore it (and wait for another time to talk).
Starved for Words	Show up on the doorstep with three ways to get the conversation started.
Punishes Through Silence	You're right, I was wrong. How can we get through this?
One-Word Answers	Prime the pump to start somewhere.
Talk to the Hand	I've hurt you. I'm sorry. Let's get past this. What can we do from here?
Eats at Me	This is hurting both of us. There is a larger issue at stake here. Let's move beyond this and work together. Here's how I suggest we proceed.

Food for Thought

Keep in mind that the other person may have been offended by someone, or something, entirely unrelated and this might not be about you at all. This could be a personal issue that's troubling that person, a health problem, or something totally unrelated. It could be a personality conflict that stemmed from an exchange at a party or a meeting that you weren't even aware of. What's important is to do your best to get to the heart of the matter and see if you can open the door. Be prepared for anything when that door opens. Keep an open mind.

BREAD & WATER DIET

Ed slaps the folder down on Terry's desk. "Have the report to me on Thursday," he says and stalks out of the cubicle. Terry is dumbfounded.

"I can't figure it out," Terry grouses to a coworker. "That's the third time this week Ed's done this. I don't know what I've done wrong but he always seems angry. He never talks to me. He just comes out here and hands me stuff to do and gives me these five- or six-word sentences. That's all I ever get. No 'Hi, hello, good morning.' Nothing! I haven't had a nice word from him in six months. I show up on time every day, I do my best work, I'm polite and respectful. I've even asked around to see if anyone else knows if I've done something to anger him, and nobody else knows, either. It's so frustrating!"

Ed's story is that he's short-staffed, overworked and under pressure to cut his budget. Everyone on the team is extremely busy, with extra projects coming in every day. He has great confidence in his team and in Terry in particular. He hates wasting Terry's time with chit-chat because he knows everyone is working hard. Consequently, he just doesn't take the time to explain every detail about every project that he gives Terry. Terry has enough to do.

Ed provides just enough information both in writing and verbally for Terry to get his job done, but clearly Terry isn't happy. If this continues, it may not be long before Terry is going to look for another job.

In a Bread & Water Diet, you get little conversation, only what minimal information you absolutely need to get by, to survive, and nothing more. You get negligible words, but no substance, no "meat," no encouragement, no support.

"Have this on my desk by Friday. There's nothing to discuss."

"Have dinner on the table by six."

"You may have ten minutes at 10 a.m. Be brief."

"You and Susan are going to work together on this one. No arguments."

"I'm buying this car for $10k. No negotiations."

You're in limbo most of the time. The hallmark of this type of diet is the absence of any kind of warmth, emotional content in the interactions, support or encouragement. This behavior can happen when someone fears a loss of power and control, losing ground or turf or maintaining authority. This often happens when an older worker perceives that the worker's job is at stake because a new employee is brought on board whose skills threaten the worker's authority or control.

It can also happen at home. Perhaps your spouse is traveling on business and has a crowded itinerary and a busy agenda. All you get is a short phone call, often on the run. The calls are emotionally distant.

"How's the weather?" "Fine."

"How was your flight?" "OK."

"Where's your hotel?" "Downtown."

This might also occur when the other person is concealing destructive behavior (spending, gambling, drinking or drugs, having an affair). He might end the conversation by pleading, "I'm tired. Can I go now?" You might find yourself cut off from conversation by avoidance, limited information, lack of cooperation or even rudeness. In any case, you're on the Bread & Water Diet, barely getting by; you know something, but not much, and it's probably making you a little crazy.

The effect of this on you could be anger if it affects your performance at work. You could be deeply frustrated if this is a loved one whom you care about, and you're worried. You could be behind schedule and you can't get the information you need and this person is hoarding a report or key data.

Food for Thought

It's very tempting when you're faced with this behavior to think that it's your fault, that you've done something to cause the problem. This is self-centered thinking. In some cases you may have done something at some point. But in many cases it's not your fault at all. It may be just that this person has an issue they're nursing and they're "singing a song." People will do this when they want the world to be all about them. They'll have a glass of wine or two and suddenly they are full of stories about how the world has victimized them. If you don't want to go down this path with them, they might move away to find someone who "really understands them"—in other words, someone who is willing to listen, or who has similar songs to sing. They can be in harmony about how the world is a victimizing place. People like this are wasting life, squandering precious time. You might be doing it yourself without realizing it. Are you "singing a song" about how the world isn't treating you the way it's supposed to? Are you feeling wronged? Perhaps it's time to stop singing and take responsibility for making the necessary changes in your own life to improve your situation.

✳ ✳ ✳

The body language associated with this behavior and also the Starvation Diet is very closed. You will see crossed arms and cold eyes. The voice tone is also cool and distant, and very professional. Time with this person is clipped and limited to only what is absolutely necessary to get the information across. Your conversations will be kept to the business at hand, nothing personal. Any attempts to reach a more intimate level of conversation will likely be quickly swept aside. Once the purpose of your interaction has been met, expect to be dismissed quickly.

Some of the fears that lurk behind this behavior include:

> *I'm losing ground. You threaten me.*

> *I have to defend my turf.*

> *The only way I can keep my job is to hoard information.*

> *I might be caught unprepared or uninformed.*

> *This is the only way I can maintain a position of power or authority.*

Some motivations that drive this behavior are:

> *I get to control your behavior, and you can't take anything away from me.*

> *You can't have access to my secrets. Stay away.*

Common negative responses to Bread & Water Diet:

> *"You have to give me more information, now."*

> *"I don't care what you (think, need, feel)."*

> *"I refuse to do anything for or with you."*

You may also get gossip and complaints behind their back, the Silent Treatment, big scenes or general lack of productivity.

HOW TO HANDLE THE BREAD & WATER DIET

Following are some behaviors to expect from the Bread & Water Diet and some suggested responses that may move people in a positive direction.

Few Words: What you get from your conversational partner is limited dialogue, and what is offered is meager fare, indeed, and certainly drained of all emotion. In this case, the best response is to offer support and reinforcement. Determine if you're the source of the fear or anger or if it's a more diffuse emotion. If you're it, find out why, and have an honest conversation about how to clear the air.

Need to Add Meat and Substance: There's a real need for sustenance to this Bread & Water Diet. The response to this thin gruel of communication is to ask for specifics and details firmly but gently, and be kind and clear. Keep asking for more information but avoid being a pest. It's important not to give up when something big is at stake: a big project, someone's performance review, or a person's health or safety. In some cases you may need to initiate an intervention.

Speak When Spoken to: You're expected to respond only when you're addressed and not initiate conversation. In this case someone is exercising power over you to maintain his position. See if you can use your power of perspective to understand if he is coming from fear, anger or retaliation from a perceived or real hurt. The appropriate response to this demand is to offer help, be of service and give suggestions that allow this person to feel in control of his destiny and situation. It may take multiple attempts to make this connection happen depending on how much pain someone is feeling or how angry this person is, especially if that anger is directed at you personally. In some cases you may have to use a third person to intervene.

Hands out Assignments with No Directions or Encouragement: You get terse emails or notes on your desk (at home, on the refrigerator) and nothing else, just marching orders for the day. The appropriate response is to find out what they're hungry for: Turf? Space? Acknowledgment? Information? See if you can provide it. What's the kind of WordFood they need from you? Is your performance lacking? Have you not been communicating appropriately? Have you done some things to lead up to this treatment?

Inaccessible: They're in a bubble and not allowing anyone to get close. They may be feeling deeply threatened by life, by circumstances, or even by you. There could have been a significant event in their life that has changed their sense of security or future at work. They may be experiencing a significant loss. They may be feeling isolated and unable to reach out. Instead of immediately judging the situation from your own viewpoint, see if you can first offer an empathetic ear to their state of mind. An appropriate response might be to see what kind of safety net you can provide for them. What is their fear? They may only need permission to speak about a personal matter with you.

Lack of Functional Conversation: They refuse to be engaged in any kind of substantial give and take. What you do get is dribble and gibberish at best, a grunt or groan, or rolled eyes and annoyance at your appearance. You may not be welcome at all when you show up at the door of your teen's bedroom. Even if you have something pressing to discuss, it may be essential to start somewhere else. The objective of your response is to make it a safe environment, steer the conversation to safe subjects and discover what's possible to talk about. Find areas of commonality, and work toward the important things. It may take you multiple conversations to do this but the payoff is worth it. You will be building trust. Again, you don't know what's going on behind the other person's protective façade.

When reaching out to someone who is providing you with the thin gruel of a Bread & Water Diet it's important to understand his or her fear or concern. Multiple servings of the care and love of HeartBreads to build trust are key. The unhealthy behavior you encounter needs to be met with the Energy Enhancers of coaching and warm guidance, offered with an open heart and caring. To someone who is fearful of loss, you offer service, not anger. You offer assistance and reassurance. Step away from your own demands and provide the safety net for this person who is probably in need and may not have the language to ask for help. By not engaging with drama, by not hiding essential information yourself and keeping your conversation open, you create an environment for trust. Provide safety and security, not more challenges, and you will likely be rewarded with an open conversation.

ASSUME THE POSITIVE INTENTION

Terry has a number of options in dealing with Ed. He doesn't know what's going on in Ed's world. Given the Bread & Water Word-Food Diet he's received, Terry has assumed the worst. He also has an opportunity to strengthen his relationship with Ed. The secret is to assume Ed's positive intention. If Ed were really out to make Terry's life miserable, he wouldn't be much of a manager. Terry can get the WordFood detail he needs by acknowledging Ed's intention to save time.

Terry can approach Ed with the following HeartBreads.

> *"Ed, if I may, I'd like to see how I can be of more help with some projects in the office. What else can I do?"*
>
> *"Ed, I appreciate the chance to work here. What can I do to be of greater service?"*
>
> *"Ed, I know you are overloaded. What else can I take on that would help? Is there anything I can do for you in particular?"*
>
> *"Ed, what kinds of concerns do you have about work projects that I can help you with right now? I'd like to be of help."*

Ed has the opportunity to learn something important about his employee as well—that he sometimes needs additional information and feedback. Terry can take the initiative and ask for coaching and direction. Terry can initiate this conversation by acknowledging Ed's positive intention before asking for Character Fiber.

> *"Ed, I appreciate your confidence in me, but I need a little more detail."*
>
> *"I could do this on my own but it would save time if you could give me some additional direction."*
>
> *"I know you would tell me if there was a problem with my work, but can you just reassure me that I'm on the right track here?"*
>
> *"I don't want to cut into your busy schedule, but could you just drop by my desk once in a while to check in?"*

Conversely, Ed could save time and improve the efficiency of his team by communicating his positive intention with phrases like:

> *"I have complete confidence in you."*

"This is right up your alley. You know more about this project than I do."

"I trust you to handle this effectively."

"You did a great job on the last project like this, so use your own judgment."

"I know you're already very busy, but I need this by Thursday. Let me know if you have any questions."

It's easy to make assumptions when we're fed either a Starvation or a Bread & Water WordFood Diet. We make up our own stories to fill in the gaps left by their silence. We can close the gap by assuming positive intention and not letting our egos get in the way. When our egos place demands on a relationship, there is no room for anyone else but ourselves. This is where there is a call for humility. We need to set the ego aside and ask, "How can we be of service? How can we help?" This creates the space for another kind of WordFood conversation. Draw from the WordFood Pyramid of HeartBreads, Energy Enhancers, Character Fiber and Balance Builders. When the ego stands aside, the WordFood Pyramid is fully functional.

Bread & Water   Responses

Few Words	Offer support and reinforcement.
Need to Add Meat and Substance	Ask for specifics and details.
Speak When Spoken to	Offer help, service and suggestions.
Hands out Assignments with No Directions or Encouragement	Find out what they're hungry for… authority? Turf? Space? See if you can provide it.
Inaccessible	What kind of safety net can you provide to them?
Lack of Functional Conversation	Make it a safe environment, discover what else is possible to talk about.

Both the Starvation and Bread & Water diets have the capacity to unload on you with anger and frustration after a period of grappling with issues privately. When you finally get these people to open up, you must be prepared for anything. They may be nursing a grudge, a fear, a hurt, and they could be in real need of a friend. It could be that their personality makes it hard for them to talk easily. You need to offer some compassion to these types of people to work through their issues as you try to reach out. Above all, remember it's not always about you. While it's tempting to think it is, there is a good possibility that something else entirely is going on and you are simply the recipient of their stress. See if you can create a safe environment for discussion. Even if you cannot, your lack of judging this person is a gift in and of itself, and that eases some of the pressure.

Food for Thought

The challenge with both the Starvation and Bread & Water diets is that you are likely already feeling left out and hurt. You may be angry, frustrated and anxious. Your challenge is to put these feelings aside as much as possible; again, sit that part of you down and show up without demands. Be present with this person who may well be in real pain. The less you bring these requirements into the conversation, the easier it will be to have a healthy WordFood exchange. The person who is willing to set aside his needs for the larger good is the one who will break the cycle and open the door. It is your graciousness and humility that bring the opportunity to connect, not anger or demands.

✳ ✳ ✳

BALLPARK DIET

Mike and Rich have been talking sports for years. Their entire friendship has been based on their mutual love of sports, and since high school they have been meeting at the local watering hole on Friday nights to discuss their passion. Neither one knows much about the other's personal life but they consider each other best friends.

When his wife, Laura, is diagnosed with breast cancer, Mike is bereft, and he feels he has nowhere to turn. He needs a friend to talk to and all he has is Rich. One Friday night he tries to open up to discuss this difficult topic with his long-time buddy. Yet, over all these years, Rich and Mike have never talked about anything but sports, and this is challenging territory. What will his friend think of him?

For his part, Rich has always enjoyed their light-hearted conversations about sports in the past. He likes Mike a lot, but wonders at times what he's like behind the sports banter. Since they've never talked about anything else, he has never pushed further. He figures that if Mike wants to discuss other topics, he'll bring them up.

People who engage you in this Ballpark Diet are focused on a single topic and that topic only, whether it's sports, technology, men, Internet, shopping, motor cross racing, the latest thing in fashion or the market ups and downs. No matter what the topic may be, somebody's "the expert." And you can count on them to know more than anyone else about it. They revel in their expertise, their know-how and the depth and breadth of their knowledge.

Some women feel isolation imposed by being an outsider when it's all about sports, when the guys at the office gather to talk about fantasy football or March Madness. They miss out on the camaraderie that is formed inside this special "club" of knowledge, stats and excitement shared by those who love the sports, grew up with sports and follow the various teams enthusiastically during the season.

Men, on the other hand, can feel left out when women form *their* own clubs and discuss shopping, fashion or children, creating impenetrable walls that guys can't enter.

The point is that whether it's a gender-based wall or not, people can cut others off by using their special proficiency to create a world where those who are not in the know aren't welcome. As youngsters we did it when we built forts or tree houses or play areas that were only for our friends and we didn't let other kids in. Gangs do it with territories. Adults do it with clubs, expertise—and conversation.

Ballpark Diets can sound like:

> *"How about the game last night?"*

> *"I have to tell you how much I saved when I bought these Louboutins!"*

> *"Jones is going to be great for Denver. Have you seen his stats?"*

> *"I just got my New York Fireman's calendar—you should see July!"*

> *"March Madness is starting this week; are we all ready?"*

> *"Macy's has some great sales going on right now… have you been yet?"*

Food for Thought

Visible and Invisible Agreements

When people get together and start developing a relationship, they form implicit agreements about how they are going to be with one another. In some cases they make verbal agreements—"visible agreements" with each other. For example, with married couples, the husband says, "Honey, I'll be home at midnight." The visible agreement is that the husband *will* be home at midnight. When he doesn't come home until 2:00 a.m., the wife is angry but says nothing. The "invisible agreement," which is the *real* binding contract, is that now that it's okay that the husband comes home at 2:00 a.m. because he wasn't called on it. Let's say this happens repeatedly over the course of a year. Every Saturday night like clockwork the husband says, and does, precisely the same thing. Says he'll be home at midnight, comes home at 2:00 a.m. The wife is angry and gets more so over time. She feels abused and put upon. Until one night, beyond patience, she changes the locks.

In this case she is in the wrong, because she has broken the contract. She has, since the beginning, implicitly agreed to the 2:00 a.m. arrival time. If she wants to change the contract she must renegotiate before he goes out that night. She must have a conversation that warns him that if he comes in at 2:00 a.m. he will find himself locked out, that she expects him in at midnight as he has said he will be, that she knows she's allowed it before, but now things are going to be different. He may well test her, but at least she has warned him. Then if he comes in at 2:00 a.m. again, he is wrong because she renegotiated.

How many visible and invisible agreements do you have in your life? How many did you try to inappropriately renegotiate and get righteous anger in return? It's not what we *say* that binds us, it's what we *do* that is the basis of the invisible, but binding, contract.

✳ ✳ ✳

Two of the characteristics of the Ballpark Diet are that the participants focus on what they know the most about and they tend to not develop beyond that expertise and into other areas of their lives. Their relationships are narrow and limited. For example, two male friends may have a lifelong relationship based on their fascination with model trains. For twenty years they have collected and built model trains, gone to conferences, and spent hours on the phone talking about their hobby. Then one day one man falls in love and his world changes overnight. He wants to discuss this with his friend but the other man feels abandoned and angry. He neither shares this interest nor is happy about this new development. In fact, he is now thinking about severing this longstanding relationship because of his friend's infatuation.

Another example is the quiet woman who says nothing at a dinner party until the conversation turns to shopping. At this point she babbles away about every aspect of how, where and when to shop for top designer deals. But when the talk turns back to work, she gets quiet once again. She is only comfortable talking about her area of expertise.

People behave like this when they don't feel they know enough about other topics in their lives. They feel that this one subject and knowledge in this one area make them an expert. They feel powerful and strong when they talk about this topic; they feel good. So they build on their expertise constantly, sometimes to the detriment of their growth.

Body language associated with this BallPark Diet can range from the intense physicality of people engaged in a passionate conversation with plenty of gesticulation to that of thoughtful people having a considered talk about their interests. They have shut out the rest of the world. What characterizes this diet is the zeal with which the participants connect with each other and keep each other in the confines of their own special universe. Others are outsiders. The BallPark Diet's eyes can get wide and express great excitement about their subject. The tone tends to be more animated and lively. For those who are more technical in their focus, you'll note a more muted expression of enthusiasm, but enthusiasm just the same. They will physically circle into a group that closes others out, as does their insiders' talk and culture. Their use of special slang, the jargon of their world, will keep others at bay like an invisible wall.

Some of the fears and concerns that are behind this diet include:

Looking foolish in other areas of their lives.

I don't know about economics, but I do know a lot about the Bears, so let's stick with football.

This is my knowledge base and I can show off about it.

I'm only smart about my obsession.

Their motivation is to be in power on their topic of expertise and to show off their breadth and depth of knowledge.

People respect my expertise. I need to stick to this topic.

The only time people notice me is when I talk about _____.

I am a thought leader in this area. I have influence.

Common negative responses to this WordFood Diet:

If you're not in the "club"...

Those (men/women) bore me

They're ridiculous. Look at what they spend their time on!

I am always left out of the conversation. I don't know anything about _____.

They intentionally talk about _____ to leave me out of the discussion. It hurts.

I'm going to make up my own group.

They're doing it on purpose to leave us out. Only those guys get the promotions around here.

If you're in the "club," here are several healthy ways to expand your influence...

Show interest in other's passions. Don't be so single minded about what you're interested in at work or play—be open minded about what others do, too.

Expand your fan club to be less exclusive of gender, age or race. No matter what your interest is, intentionally or unintentionally leaving others out can be hurtful to people who are genuinely interested. Be watchful for those on the sidelines looking in. Be willing to educate, include, inform and motivate those who are feeling a little left out.

Notice how your "club" is costing performance. Sometimes your enthusiasm about sports or shopping can get engaging at work, and involve a lot of time and energy. Be mindful of how this will impact other's performances. While it may be fun for a while, it does hurt their status with their own superiors, if not your position with your own, unless your superior is part of your "club." Be responsible.

Take it out of the office. If your "club" eats up significant work time, it's time to move it to a local watering hole after hours. And it's also time to notice who gets left behind when this happens. If this means excluding some key people, it might be time to disband, or invite them along.

WHAT TO EXPECT FROM THIS DIET

Here are some behaviors that you can expect from the Ballpark Diet, and a few appropriate positive WordFood responses to try.

Can Only Connect on One Topic: Sports, shopping, work, technology, etc. One appropriate response would be to learn to speak that language and join the club. Be part of the party. Sometimes it doesn't hurt to expand your vocabulary and take a seat at the table. This could broaden your friendships or improve your relationship substantially.

One Dimensional: The focus is always on a single issue, and delving deep into that issue. You get beleaguered with stats, details and information *ad nauseum*. An appropriate response would be to explore the outside boundaries of the knowledge and find areas of commonality where you can make a contribution. Acknowledge their expertise, be complimentary, and then move out to the edges with them.

How 'bout Dem Bears: They have a competitive, join-my-team approach, expecting you to jump on board and cheer for their team. One response would be to take the opposite view to develop contention to liven things up. This makes them think twice about their propensity to enlist everyone around them to their cause, and it invites a discussion instead of complete agreement.

Can't Talk about Feelings: In many cases, people who are wrapped up in a single issue are burying something else. They use their expertise and knowledge to mask other emotions and personal issues. The response might be to challenge them about a hot topic in their area of expertise to get them excited, and then explore their viewpoint and move gently into other areas. What else are they passionate about? What else matters to them? It's worth it to see where you can go on the edges of the comfort zone.

Another way to go is explore with them what they might be doing if they didn't have this passion. What else might they get involved in? What options might they explore? Suggest that it's just for the sake of discussion, but that there is the possibility of another life without this obsession.

Wants You in Their Fan Club: They're enlisting! These people want you to be part of their excitement and their love of sports, or shopping, the Internet or whatever has captured their full attention. Your involvement will underscore their belief that they are right about how great it is, and how right they are that it's the best thing for them. The appropriate response would be to stay on the periphery and enjoy the energy, but keep from being sucked in. You can certainly validate their enthusiasm without jumping on their bandwagon. If anything, a certain slowing down of that energy might be appropriate if it's having a negative effect on other workers or family members.

If a husband is addicted to gardening and his wife is left out for lack of interest, she's not going to become the world's next expert on exotic roses. The same is true with her and the football she loves; he's not going to become an expert on the 49ers. But each *could* make a move toward involvement in their spouse's world, show an interest and take steps toward being included so that they are spending time with their spouse. Conversely, they can ask their spouse to do the same with them. If their spouse is wholly unwilling, finding something else to do that creates common ground is helpful.

With the Ballpark Diet, each of the four Pyramid groups is involved. You need lots of servings of HeartBreads to build trust and regard. This helps those who are operating out of a fear of not knowing enough, or being enough of an expert in anything other than that one topic. Appeal to those who have a great deal of confidence to teach others, but also to expand their world to learn more. The Energy Enhancers provide compliments to develop greater confidence about their skills and abilities. The Character Fiber mentoring builds the mental toughness to take on bigger challenges in life, more topics and more relationships outside their comfort zone. This also helps set boundaries about how much time is spent on the topic during time spent together. Character Fiber will help people see that life has many more spheres of interest. People can be reached through those spheres, and more friends are made when you have more interests. Balance Builders are appropriate for those who are arrogant about their knowledge and who tend to use it to exclude others from their private "club." Balance Builders guide the extreme behaviors of those who have hurt others by their exclusionary behavior. This also helps guide those who have impacted work performance or have demonstrated isolationist behavior or hurt others at the office.

CHANGING THE CONVERSATION

Mike, the sports enthusiast, needs to reach out to Rich in a new way to invite him to participate at a deeper level. He can try using a combination of Energy Enhancers and HeartBreads to start the conversation and build the bridge to ask for help. He probably has no idea that Rich is actually open to the idea of expanding the relationship and all he has to do is ask:

> *"Rich, you're my best friend. I always enjoy your company better than anyone else's. You're smarter than anyone else I know. I need your smarts right now."*

> *"Rich, I really appreciate the time we spend together. You're a super guy and I trust your opinion. That's why I need your opinion on something important."*

> *"Rich, I'd like to change the subject tonight. We usually talk sports, but I'd like to discuss something different because I need your insights. May I do that?"*

In this case, Mike is giving Rich the chance to say no, which respects Rich's role in a long-standing relationship. Rich may not want to change how they talk. In this scenario, however, Rich has an interest. He can offer:

> *"Mike, you and I have always discussed sports. But if there's something else you'd like to discuss, I'm open to that."*

> *"I don't mind talking about something else if it's important to you."*

> *"If you have another topic to discuss, go right ahead. How can I help?"*

Rich is letting Mike know that he is willing to discuss something new. He's there to be Mike's friend. In this case, Mike has simply never tested the boundaries of Rich's friendship, and he's fortunate that Rich is open to the idea.

Not everyone will be willing to do this with you. You need to respect existing boundaries and establish new ones before you can crash the gates with something unexpected that could potentially end the relationship. Ask permission to renegotiate your invisible agreements first. You may discover you've made unfair assumptions about how others feel about your relationship, and new doors may open to your exchanges.

Ballpark Responses

Can Only Connect on One Topic: sports, shopping, work, technology	Learn to speak that language: join the club.
One Dimensional	Explore the outside boundaries of the knowledge and find related areas of commonality.
Hey, How 'bout Dem Bears	Take the opposite view and develop contention and get things livened up.
Can't Talk about Feelings	Challenge about hot topic and get them riled, and then explore their viewpoint.
Wants You in Their Fan Club	Join, be part of their party.

Uncomfortable if You Change the Subject or Probe	Do it subtly, allow them to be the "expert" where you guide them.
Wants a Fan Club About His/her Obsession	Stay on the periphery, enjoy the energy but keep from getting sucked in.

Food for Thought

New Wine in Old Bottles

What happens when someone feeds us brand new WordFood? Perhaps this WordFood could help us grow and become someone new and wonderful? How do we receive this information? Are we open to it?

All too often when we take in new WordFood we filter it through old mental processes, trying to fit it into earlier ways of thinking. We force it to fit old paradigms. We totally miss the message—and the opportunity to grow and become someone new and wonderful through exposure to new ideas and concepts.

Have you ever gone to a high school reunion having lost a lot of weight or changed yourself in some significant way, only to be met by your old acquaintances with the same nicknames or greetings as you did back in high school? It's as though they didn't give you permission to change. It's painful to be locked into that persona forever. You're the fat kid, the geek, the shy girl.

No matter who you have become today, others still see you as you were. Of course, parents always see us as their kids and have a hard time seeing us as the adults we have become.

Have you ever done this to a friend who has gone through a significant change? Someone who has made a personal shift of some kind and who has looked to you for acknowledgment? How long did it take for you to actually see and recognize this change, especially if it wasn't a physical one? Sometimes we don't give our friends—or our family—permission to be other than how we have always seen them. We like them as they are; predictable, good old Harry or Mary. It's uncomfortable when stodgy Aunt Edna shows up in a snazzy red convertible, sporting a cute young boyfriend. Or fat Fred shows up one hundred pounds lighter and tanned, looking like a million bucks. It's a shock. They no longer fit our picture of who they should be. That's when the well-intentioned mother starts shoving fatty foods in front of Fred to make him eat, right after he's just spent the last year disciplining himself to lose the weight.

We do this to ourselves. We lock in who we think we are and effectively close the gate to anything new. When we hear new WordFood that invites us to shift or change, it hits this Who-I-Am filter and gets sorted accordingly. It's tough to hear new concepts or ideas that challenge our notion of who we are. But then, we consider this idea, try it on for size, even adapt to the new behavior or idea as our own. It takes courage, and the ability to step outside our everyday thinking to do it.

Can you, will you, step outside the safe, everyday norm, to challenge your thinking when you are faced with something new? Instead of discarding new WordFood outright, will you take a moment and ask, "What can I learn from this? How can this help me grow?"

Every day, in some way, we are being offered new wine in the form of WordFood. Are you forcing it into old bottles? How can you take advantage of what's being offered?

There's always the possibility that something amazing may happen.

"When you are inspired by some great purpose, some extraordinary project, all your thoughts break their bonds. Your mind transcends limitations, your consciousness expands in every direction, and you find yourself in a new, great and wonderful world."

—The Yoga Sutras of Patanjali

MEAT & POTATOES DIET

Jan Hoffstetler has been the manager of a branch of First National Bank for more than twenty-five years. She's an institution there, and everyone loves her and the way she does business. She considers herself the best customer service person in the region, and for good reason. She's won every award in the bank, year after year. The bank is proud of her and she's been proud to be with First National. That is, until First National got bought out by United Trust and they started putting in this new sales system. All of a sudden she's expected to start pushing sales. New fees for everything. Fees on things she always gave her customers for free, like traveler's checks for little old ladies going to Florida. What is she supposed to tell her little old lady friends now? They certainly won't appreciate the impact on their limited incomes.

Jan is responsible for training all the tellers and customer service reps at her branch. She doesn't approve of the new emphasis on sales. She believes that when customers come to the bank they know exactly what they want. Jan feels that she is going to turn into a used car salesperson by trying to sell some poor customer five new products just because they walked in and sat down. That's the new program United Trust is pushing.

Well, not Jan. She's not going to tell any of her tellers or customer service reps to do it either. At her branch, business is going to be done the old fashioned way. In time, United Trust will see things her way. She's sure of it, and that's how she wants to keep on training her employees, too.

Jan's regional manager, David, is under pressure to make sure that the new system is up and running. He knows that Jan is resisting. He also knows how popular she is with the customers and the staff. But times have changed, and so must Jan. If she doesn't adapt to the new program, he will have to let her go, along with any other members of the staff who refuse to learn this new program.

People on a Meat & Potatoes Diet are very comfortable where they are. They don't like change, they like things to be predictable for years to come. They want the same food, the same routines, the same people, the same clothing, and the same drive to work every day. They don't like it when new software is installed, or if their spouse decides to change a hairstyle or start a new exercise program. They're threatened by changes at the office or plant. They may resist training on diversity and sensitivity about age, race and gender, and refuse to take responsibility for their own microinequities. And they will hunker down and resist changes and undermine them when they happen.

People on a Meat & Potatoes WordFood Diet prefer normalcy and predictability. When routines change, this threatens their sense of well being, and they will react out of fear of a loss of their place in the world as they know it, whether it's a loss of turf, power, place or friends. Their resistance can take any number of forms. They may undermine the boss or the system, refuse to cooperate, and act with passive resistance or organize a union.

Meat & Potatoes people may make themselves large, or puff themselves up self-righteously to make their point. Their body language conveys, "I'm right and you're wrong" or "You can't make me." They are likely to cross their arms and close off discussion. They will probably hold eye contact but with anger and forcefulness, even trying to stare you down. This group can be defensive, bullish and sanctimonious. Or they may resort to whining and a poor-me approach, or curl up into themselves in self-pity. They may go hide out in their "cave," their office or garage or bedroom, to get away from the demands of life. They may bury themselves in busy work to avoid dealing with the issue at hand.

Their fear is driven by a lack of safety or normalcy. People who are on the Meat & Potatoes Diet fear the unknown, the new and different. They don't want Thai Chicken Salad or Gnocchi: they want Meat & Potatoes—every night at 6:00, with the dog at their feet, just like last night.

> *"Don't change the routine. You do, and you'll have trouble."*
>
> *"I like things just the way they are."*
>
> *"What's the matter with how I do things now?"*
>
> *"Change things and I'll undermine the program."*
>
> *"Why don't you buy our regular salad dressing?"*
>
> *"I want to watch our favorite program, not this stuff."*
>
> *"Do you have to change our menu on Friday nights? I like meat loaf."*
>
> *"I don't like your new hairstyle. I liked it the old way."*
>
> *"The software program is just fine like it is. We don't need a new one."*
>
> *"Honey, don't lose weight. I like your muffin top."*
>
> *"But I like going to Florida every year for vacation!"*

Their motivation is to reduce stress, reduce risk maintain sameness, routine and predictability. Control of their environment is paramount.

> *"Don't show me something different or bring in new systems, a new boss or diversity training!"*
>
> *"Keep things just as they are and we'll be just fine."*

"Don't give me some young kid telling me what to do."

Common negative responses to this WordFood Diet:

"Can't teach old dogs new tricks."

"Those managers are too predictable, and they're not trainable."

"Those women can't change. They're not salvageable in the new system."

"For them, there's nothing ventured outside the norm."

"They're just bigots and misogynists. They will never change."

WHAT TO EXPECT FROM THE MEAT & POTATOES DIET

The behaviors below are associated with the Meat & Potatoes Diet. You'll also find some suggestions to help you get a more positive response from this group.

Nothing Ventured: These people are in lockstep with their methods and happy with the way things are. Despite the organization's movement to make changes, there is no desire to change anything at all. The appropriate response might be guidance and explanation. Provide a safe environment and value their contributions so far, but make it clear that things are shifting and you want them on board. Ask them how they would like to be included. Involve them in the new activities if they are willing. Ask their advice.

Know What You'll Always Get: You get totally predictable behavior in every situation. The response could be to express their value but also the need for adaptation. Let them vent and express their fears in full. Don't argue or interrupt, let them get it all out, and then explain the situation and the value to them of the new situation. Here it's important to allow them to openly express their concern about how they have to change and how much they might resent it. Let them talk about what they're losing or the thing they might be losing. Don't argue; just be a listening post. Sometimes that's all that is necessary. Again, don't make it all about you. You don't always have to respond when people vent, and you may not have the answers anyway. Just let the anger or fear express itself, and then see if it's time to move to a more constructive conversation. Be sure you take the time to value what they have done for the company or the relationship before suggesting what needs to come next.

Stuck in a Rut, Don't Rock the Boat: They are deeply committed to one way of doing things. They could have been with the company or in a marriage for many years, and have been perfectly comfortable with the status quo. Here you or the company comes along with a big change, and this could be shattering their world or sense of self. Take into account how big an impact this might have on other people. You may have taken a lot of time to think about this change and have accepted it but it may be brand-new news to other people. Empathize by remembering how you first reacted to the news, and how long it took you to adjust.

An effective approach would be to acknowledge the fear or potential fear, show value of adaptation of new skills or waysof doing things with small changes, nothing radical right away. More than anything, honor the fact that there is a sea of change going on and that needs to be dealt with, and it's not going to happen overnight. There needs to be some assistance with this process, and a go-get-'em attitude isn't the kind of help that is needed right now. Genuine concern, care, listening and openness are absolutely key. Understanding from you that you recognize that this information could be difficult for them and also hard for them to handle could be very helpful.

Addicted to Safety, Security: People who like the Meat & Potatoes Diet have a real fear of letting go of past ways of doing things. An approach might be to provide coaching, helping them to adapt to the new order of things. What's needed here is a sensitive ear, not the kind of enthusiastic, get-with-the-program coaching appropriate to a sports team. What's called for is real listening to the concerns, the fears, the genuine misgivings these people have about what they are losing through the changes they are experiencing, how threatened they are, and how they may be getting left behind. There is a reason for their behavior. Find out what that reason is. Pushing for performance and trying to force change is only going to be met with more resistance.

Another key strategy is to ensure that these people are making connections with others and forming supportive networks. During times of change most people go into hiding and stop talking to others, feel sorry for themselves or form pity parties in which they engender bad feelings. Finding new relationships and groups to join and creating positive connections can help them adjust to the new reality. The single most important adaptive strategies during transitions are networking and forming new relationships. Whether it's to ease the sense of isolation or to break up the negative groups that form to undermine what management is trying to accomplish, it helps to move people forward. Encourage them to make new friends, join or form new groups. While both of these enterprises mean taking new steps, they are critical to ending isolation, loneliness and the self-imposed self-righteousness that comes from the feeling of being singled out during a transition period.

Unaware of Microinequities: In some cases, these folks can be resistant to the notion that what they do every day could be offensive to some people. "This is the way I've always treated people" may be their answer, or "Just deal with it" could be another. An approach would be to educate them about microinequities and give plenty of examples that touch their own personal experience. Help them see how they themselves have been mistreated so that they have a perspective on how it feels to be slighted. Instead of making them wrong, help them feel the other person's discomfort and gain insight. Often, seeing things from someone else's viewpoint is enough to make a significant difference and help change this person's perspective about microinequities and, possibly, their behavior. Creating an open discussion or forum with under-represented groups in a safe environment can help open eyes.

Not Willing to Take Risks of Any Kind: This behavior comes from many years in a series of habitual behavior, predictable routines, no challenges to their authority or other situations that haven't encouraged any real personal growth. Now perhaps they are facing the first significant challenge of their profession-al or personal lives, whether it's at work or home. An approach would be to educate them about the transition process, provide guidance and coaching through the transition and develop their skills and knowledge about dealing with change. Introduce new healthy "foods" a little at a time. People who have never been challenged are going to take challenge hard, so don't expect Meat & Potatoes Diet people to embrace changes with open arms. They have to see the benefits. Threats only make things worse, especially if dealing with unions.

There is a need for all four groups from the Pyramid for this com-munity of people. First, plenty of the caring HeartBreads to build trust and collaboration so you can create the conversation. This is a group that may feel deeply threatened by change, so a real need exists for a sense of safety that is engendered by listening and developing their self-worth.

The reinforcement and acknowledgment that comes from Energy Enhancers are crucial to help them through the transition period. They will need caring support and guidance to help them see the contributions they can make to the organization or to the relationship.

Character Fiber will provide a sense of safety through the change period and provide a safe place to vent their concerns and frustrations, which is an essential part of the transition process. This is the coaching that will help them see the value of networking and making new connections to get through their transition.

Another strategy to help those on a Meat & Potatoes Diet is to get them engaged to coach other employees. This enlists them in the overall corporate agenda, makes them responsible for their own growth and further helps them feel important to the new world where they have a place. Having this kind of a role allows them to make a key contribution to the corporation, while simultaneously helping them process through their concerns and misgivings.

Finally, Balance Builders are important where there are issues with microinequities or inappropriate behaviors in areas of diversity. This kind of direct coaching brings out the extremes of anger—or fear-based behavior—that is deeply dysfunctional at the workplace, or that is damaging a marriage or partnership. It may be appropriate at this point to bring in a third party to act as an impartial observer or counselor. An angry employee could do real damage during a delicate time in a company's transition or merger, and a hurt divorcing spouse can do terrible damage to children. Think love, not lawyers.

BRIDGE TO THE FUTURE

Jan Hoffstetler is likely to have challenges quickly with United Trust if she doesn't align with the program. As valuable as she has been for the past twenty-five years, this is a new company, with new programs and new standards for performance. Her supervisor David can use a combination of HeartBreads, Energy Enhancers and Character Builders to make the case:

> "Jan, you have been an extremely valuable employee here."

> "You're going to continue to make contributions, but in a different way."

> "Your leadership is going to be critical to helping us succeed."

> "We will help you translate the message to your customers and your employees about the fees."

> "We see ways that you can coach your employees to perform in the new system to succeed."

> "Jan, I will be available to you to help you work through this transition time of getting used to the new program."

> "Jan, you know I appreciate all you have done here and I don't want to lose your skills and contribution."

Jan now has the option of asking for assistance instead of resisting everything that the bank is asking her to do.

> "David, what is the role you're willing to play in my future with the bank?"

"I'm concerned about losing our customers because of the fees. What am I going to tell them so that we don't watch them go to another bank?"

"David, I want to feel as though I can still make a difference in this new program. What can I do to help?"

"I'm not comfortable with the changes but perhaps you can help me."

Meat & Potatoes	Responses
Nothing Ventured	Guidance and explanation—provide a safe environment and value their contributions so far.
Know What You'll Always Get	Express their value but also the need for adaptation. Let them vent and express fears.
Predictable Daily Routines	Value for consistency, praise and express need for similar contribution but in a new environment.
Stuck in a Rut, Don't Rock the Boat	Acknowledge fear or potential fear, show value of adaptation of new skill or way of doing things with micro changes.
Addicted to Safety, Security	Coaching, help them adapt, networks.

Unaware of Microinequities	Educate about microinequities, give examples in their own experience.
No Risks	Educate about transition process, change, coach through neutral zone and develop skills through process.

Food for Thought

A lot of fear lurks behind the behavior in the Meat & Potatoes Diet. This is a group that deserves compassion and patience through change and the transition period, and the recognition that they have invested a great deal of themselves into a relationship, whether it's a marriage or a job. That deserves to be honored. In many cases, what's needed to move forward is simply to let them express their hurt, anger and frustration about their losses. It is the same grieving process invoked by death and dying, and involves some of the same emotions—whether it's the loss of a position, a major change at work, a divorce, a child leaving the home or other major change. Something is being lost and needs to be acknowledged. This group will benefit from the support of networks at the same time they are likely to be isolating themselves or surrounding themselves with people who are poisoning them. Try to involve them with networks of new people and new friends who can bring positive outlooks and positive energy into their lives and a much more caring environment for them.

Some who are on a Meat & Potatoes Diet just want to be right about how you are wrong to make changes. You may not be able to sway these people to your way of thinking. You have to recognize that sometimes people are just angry, stupid, stubborn, mean or committed to being ugly. It's not up to you to fix them. Do your best and move on.

This is true for all the diets. While it's important to have compassion, it's also very important to know when to draw the line at trying to fix folks. Some just don't want your help, and they are quite happy being broken. Sometimes WordFood isn't going to work at all despite your best efforts because the person you're talking to is just plain rotten. Your first responsibility is to yourself and when you start paying a price for trying to work with others, it's time to let go.

ICE CREAM & CAKE DIET

Name a party in Washington, DC and Sarah is there. Name an important person in the room and she is draped on his arm, whispering in his ear, using honeyed tones, currying favor. Point out a more important person across the room and she is there in a heartbeat, fawning all over this new person, hugging and air kissing. Sarah knows little about personal space or boundaries. She wants to be seen, be acknowledged and be noticed. She wants the world to see her with all the right people. Whether it's a political or corporate party, Sarah does her best to make herself the center of attention, through her clothing, looks and actions. She is impossible to ignore and, for many people, challenging to deal with. She gets what she wants through manipulation and wheedling, and sometimes by setting people against each other. She uses information as currency, always building a bank of it to use for and against people, but always for her own protection. The problem is, Sarah is Bill's employee. Bill is her new boss, and her behavior is an embarrassment to him. She is a capable public relations executive and lobbyist, but her excesses don't reflect well on the corporation's conservative reputation. Bill has to have a serious talk with Sarah, and soon.

When Sarah comes on to people she uses phrases like:

> *"Darling, it is SOOOOO good to see you! You're my dearest of friends!"*

> *"Sweetie, I missed you SOOOOOO much, you're my closest buddy, mwah!"*

> *"Sweetheart, you're the best! I am so delighted you're here, we just HAVE to talk…"*

> *"Honey, I've been dying to see you, you're my favorite person in the world!"*

"Wait until I tell you what I heard about Susan."

"I've got the latest gossip on Allen—did you know that he's cheating on Jan?"

"You know I'd never tell anyone about your secret!"

The truth is that Sarah is very insecure about her abilities, and she is doing what she thinks works best in this environment. Her extremes reflect how scared she often feels about her ability to do her job.

Bill, her boss, is concerned. While he respects the skills she has, her propensity for inappropriate fawning on senior executives has gone overboard and he needs to rein her in.

People on the Ice Cream & Cake Diet tend to lay on the compliments and sweetness, and come on to those around them like gangbusters. They try to connect too quickly and sometimes inappropriately. They can be flatterers and they are aggressively friendly, enthusiastic and affectionate, to the brink of overwhelm. They may touch or hug in situations where it embarrasses people. They can also be politically inclined rather than authentic in their communications. You might not always know whom you're talking to with people who fall into this group. What's their agenda? This Word-Food Diet is so rich that it can make people gag a little.

The Ice Cream & Cake Diet people are hungry for attention. They tend to dress flamboyantly, live out loud, and be found at all the best parties in town. On a large scale, they are likely found on the society pages and the gossip columns and have scads of pictures of themselves with celebrities on the walls, desk and credenzas and all over Facebook. They are name-droppers, and their networks are broad and deep. They can call in a favor from just about anyone, be invited to stay at innumerable houses in a number of big cities across the world.

On a smaller scale, they dress to impress, fawn all over people and are social climbers. They will express friendship in their faces but their eyes are often blank or disengaged, or looking across the room for their next mark. Their vocal tone is also flattering. You may hear lots of apparent warmth but there may be an undertone of falseness. Listen for it. You may hear many claims to your history of friendship when you've only known each other for a few days. These people will shake your hand and not look you in the eye but they'll be on to the next person in seconds.

There may be laughter with a false ring to it, a lot of gaiety and hilarity and lots of friends around, but in the bright light of morning this Ice Cream & Cake Diet can be all alone. Or, the opposite may be true; they are always surrounded by people and impossible to get alone to have a genuine conversation with, by design. There may be an "everything's wonderful" quality to their conversation, and a lack of reality to their interactions, because their world is all about imagery, impressions and misapprehensions. They may constantly pull you aside "for a word." This is to build confidences, but they're doing it with everyone else as well.

The fears that drive this diet include:

> *Everyone has to love me!*
>
> *I'm not attractive enough.*
>
> *Everyone has to approve of me!*
>
> *I've got to run my game.*
>
> *I've got to get that promotion no matter what.*
>
> *This campaign is mine to win.*
>
> *I'm the belle of the ball; everyone is in my pocket tonight.*

Their sticky sweet compliments constitute empty calories for they are based in fear behaviors; they don't come from confidence. Their motivations may include:

> *I want you in my fan club.*
>
> *I want you to publicly approve of me.*
>
> *I want you to talk well of me to others.*
>
> *Please just be nice to me.*
>
> *Please support my cause (and me by way of it).*
>
> *I'm terribly lonely!*
>
> *I have to look important!*
>
> *My agenda is more important than yours.*

They may also be motivated by genuine affection and the desire to connect, but when this behavior becomes toxic in its excesses, its origins are from fear. Or, they can be motivated by pure ambition, and could care less about you or your feelings. They are using you as a stepping-stone and you are simply in their way as they head to the top.

Negative responses to this diet:

> *"She makes me really uncomfortable."*
>
> *"She's all over me all the time."*
>
> *"She's always flitting around, flirting with everyone."*
>
> *"Her constant touching embarrasses me."*
>
> *"I flat out don't trust her intentions."*
>
> *"I need to get away from her!"*

WHAT TO EXPECT FROM THE ICE CREAM & CAKE DIET

Some of the behaviors you can expect from people on this diet are presented below along with some suggestions about how to respond to them.

Flattery: People on this diet are great flatterers. You may find yourself on the receiving end of many compliments that may get to the point of gushing. An appropriate response would be to make a call to frankness. You needn't be rude, just gently close the gushing faucet and get to the conversation at hand. You might ask, "What do you really need from me?"

Gossip: These people try to engage you in gossip. Your best response is to not participate. Either politely move on to another person or stop the conversation and gently change the subject. If they persist, walk away, while recognizing you may be the topic of their next attack.

Political Maneuvering: You're in the middle of what is clearly some organizing that you're not comfortable with and you want out. An appropriate response is to not be party to what you sense may be unethical behavior and be clear about your intentions. Be gracious in your exit—don't assume anything. Simply move away from the conversation.

Overwhelm: You feel totally overcome by their approach. They have come on way too strong, whether it's a sales pitch for something, they're being too flattering, they're standing too close to you— whatever it is, it's just too much. Step back from the onslaught and ask for a slowdown. Regroup, and ask for clarity. Be kind but be clear. You have a right to your personal space. Remember that they could have issues around being loved and accepted and they aren't terribly respectful of boundaries. It's up to you to re-establish those boundaries for them so that you can have a valuable conversation that works for everyone. This is an excellent moment in which you all can grow.

Hail Fellow, Well Met: Someone has accosted you loudly, and you feel as though it's all about impressions for the crowd rather than sincerity. In fact, he's looking around the room instead of at you, while all this greeting is going on. A positive response could be to slow him down, pull him aside and engage him quietly and personally. Ask him what he wants to talk to you about one on one, how can you be of service? What can you do for him? This is a direct question that may place him in a very different state of mind, and one that makes him think differently—and more responsibly.

Positive response: healthy WordFood for a healthy diet. These people need servings from all four WordFood Groups of the Pyramid. Since they seek approval and love, HeartBreads are paramount to building confidence. Compassion is the key to understanding their need to be liked and to get approval. They need to be dealt with graciously, not with frustration or anger, as that will escalate the sticky sweetness and attempts to convince that are their calling card. They require patience and warmth over time and honest acceptance of their authentic selves, which might not be obvious initially as their personas are well developed.

When threatened, Ice Cream & Cake Diets can engage in gossip or ill will, so an unwillingness to participate in these toxic behaviors is essential. Energy Enhancers provide the life-affirming compliments that this group so needs to feel valued.

Character Fiber builds this group's backbone. These people need to be challenged and developed to stand on their own. People on an Ice Cream & Cake Diet need to believe in themselves, to not need a cause to define themselves. They need to understand they don't have to be sycophants to survive. Character Fiber provides the feedback and development so these folks don't need to flatter to fly on their own. This does not apply to those on this diet with an agenda to take advantage of others for their own ambition, however. These people have plenty of backbone, and they can be quick to cut and slash where necessary to get where they're going.

Because Ice Cream & Cake Diets can go to extremes, servings of Balance Builders are sometimes necessary when their behavior is inappropriate. Toxic gossip, maneuvering that can cause harm, buttering up that is clearly a setup, all have to be addressed. All these behaviors need to be called out for what they are: fear based. However, if someone in this group has achieved something significant, it's important to heap compliments on them, for this is what they most hunger for. If it's well deserved, serve a platter full.

People on an Ice Cream & Cake Diet are hungry for recognition and acknowledgment. They need to be loved and accepted in a deeply elemental way. Anger or resentment directed at them only deepens the problem. It's critically important to understand that it's not about you, it's about helping them realize their value and giving them breathing space. Don't judge their frailty. In conversations with this group of approval hounds, be gentle when you set boundaries. Expressions of anger are taken way out of proportion and exaggerated. Your patience and tenderness are truly called for in these exchanges.

HANDLE WITH CARE

Sarah is, at first blush, high maintenance. But she is worth reaching, and it's going to take a little work to find the person hiding behind the public persona.

To talk to Sarah you need to confront where she uses her mask to hide so effectively. She is likely to deflect initial attempts to be honest and frank, as it is Energy Enhancers needed to build her habit to avoid openness. Her mask is firmly in place. You will need confidence and also Character Fiber to get her out of her element and away from the busy public environments where she can flit from person to person as is her habit and her escape. Get her to sit down and be present with you—this will be hard for her.

When you speak to Sarah, acknowledge her with warmth and validate the things she does well. Compliment her, and then speak to her honestly about her behavior.

> *What does she do well that is working? How does she positively represent the company?*

> *Where are there areas of improvement? And how can you help her?*

You may get breezy brush-offs or denials here, where the persona has difficulty receiving feedback. Stick with it. Be firm and be kind. People in this diet have a very hard time hearing anything negative. Ask:

> *How can you provide coaching and mentoring to help guide the behavior?*

> *If it has gone way off track, what are you willing to do to set some tough guidelines that have to be followed?*

> *You may get tears, as this is a diet type that is easily hurt. Or at least it's easy for them to act as-if. Tears can also be manipulative. Be empathetic but stand your ground. You have an expectation that behavior will change for the better.*

It's possible that she will have a battery of protective devices to keep her mask in place and to keep you from seeing or experiencing her more authentic self, which she fears isn't acceptable. She may never reveal these aspects to you. Sarah's behavior is a highly developed coping mechanism borne out of pain, and it won't be dislodged overnight. If she is an otherwise valued and capable employee, then you will want to continue to invest in her development. Just recognize that helping her find her authentic voice may take a third party's guidance, and it may be time to help her find a mentor or counselor.

> *"Sarah, you are really skilled at your lobbying and PR work. We're proud of you. You might want to tone down layering it on with people."*

> *"Sarah, your people skills are so good that you don't need to try so hard. You can be your authentic self— and people will like you even more."*

> *"Sarah, you're very capable and I value your contribution here. You can do even more if you work to develop a gracious distance with our clients."*

> *"I know you can develop this new skill set. You're very smart."*

Sarah, whose antennae are highly developed, may well know that Bill is irked by something. She may ask him:

> *"Bill, would you please let me know your feedback on my performance?"*

> *"Bill, I'd value your input on how I can do a better job for the company."*

> *"I'm concerned I may not be living up to your expectations. What can I do differently?"*

> *"I could use your guidance on the IBM account. What do you think my strategy should be?"*

Ice Cream & Cake	Responses
Flattery	Make a call to frankness and be gracious for a call to honesty.
Lay It on a Little Thick	Cut to the chase and be direct.
Butter Up	Respond with silence, or compliment with sincerity and truth and move on.
Gossip	Don't participate—either move on or stop the conversation and change the subject.
Political Maneuvering	Don't be party to unethical behavior and be clear about your intentions.
Overwhelm	Step back from the onslaught and ask for a slowdown, regroup and ask for clarity.
Hail Fellow, Well Met	Slow them down and engage them.

Ice Cream & Cake Diet people are so starved for love, it's wise to keep in mind that disapproval and anger will backfire. It's also important to remember that in some cases, love can disappear into them like a Black Hole because they've been emotionally damaged at some point. A great deal of patience is called for, and understanding that many in this group are operating out of pain and a real fear of not being enough. Make the environment as safe as possible when you call for clarity. Make them feel appreciated, not ridiculed—ridicule is toxic. Chances are they've had their share of this already and what you're being fed is a coping mechanism. These coping skills can be very useful in some quarters. Draw your boundaries with gentility and understanding. These people look in the mirror and do not like what they see. They look for all their validation outside themselves.

Another aspect of this WordFood Diet is whining to get their way. Like a child who wants a treat, this group can be very demanding about what they want. Keep in mind their motivations and respond to the behavior in an adult way. Don't give in or it will reinforce the negative trait.

This is a diet where third party intervention may well be called for. A mentor, a coach, a guidance counselor or spiritual counselor would be a good investment. Because it is so challenging to get people on this diet to be authentic with themselves, much less with you, this group needs a caring and nonjudgmental ear. They also need someone who will help them be less harsh on themselves. These are areas where professional help comes in.

Make sure you differentiate those who are functioning out of fear and those who are pure operators. This latter group has to be called out for what they are—people who have agendas where others stand to lose. They are political animals and they take no prisoners. There is no such thing as harmless gossip with them. You're better off removing them from your employ if possible, as these operators are toxic to the organization as well as themselves.

Food for Thought

All of us wish to be discovered and recognized. We all wish to be loved and accepted for who we really are, not for the masks that we put forth into the world. However, many if not most of us have a protective face we wear for the public, a more "acceptable" persona, which we present for general consumption. Especially for people on an Ice Cream & Cake Diet, this persona may be a significantly different person from who we really are, and we are well aware that, when someone finds out the difference, it may surprise them.

Often people have developed powerful coping mechanisms for extreme shyness or disabilities by adapting strong personality traits, which cover up what they think would otherwise cripple them in the public eye. Over time the mechanism comes to define who they are. They have adapted so well that the shyness is either forgotten or the disability is extremely well hidden. But the internal persona is still aware, and possibly still deeply affected by that knowledge. It is this persona that drives the external behaviors—the fear of being discovered and not liked as a result.

When someone displays the extreme WordFood of Ice Cream & Cake, or similar adaptive behaviors, it is kind to keep in mind that there is someone behind the mask who wishes to be received as is. While it probably won't work to confront that person directly, not responding too harshly to his or her extremes is sometimes enough. There perhaps may be a child inside who was at one point deemed undesirable and this is how that person copes with that pain. You may not be able to heal the hurt but you needn't add to it, and you can indeed soothe it with kindness. And isn't that what we all want?

DEVIL'S FOOD DIET

Jason was an operations manager for a large corporation in Kansas City. He has an MBA, a wife, a stepson and a suburban house with an upper middle-class lifestyle. He's very bright, with every reason to be happy about his prospects in the world. Until the economy cost him his job, that is. That's when things went from bad to worse in his world. He began to listen when his friends told him that it was the U.S. president's fault that he was out of a job. He began to get involved with groups that had strong beliefs that the president would "come get their guns and put them all on a reservation somewhere" so Jason began stockpiling food and guns at his home. His wife began drinking heavily, gaining weight and withdrawing. Their stepson, already a problem, became worse. Jason's brother George made every attempt to reason with him, provide logical perspectives, love and understanding. He offered to help rewrite Jason's resume, help him find a new job. But George worked for the very government that Jason had decided was the enemy, and Jason refused his help.

Jason has become more and more steeped in the anti-government rhetoric. Instead of looking for a new job and finding ways to solve his problems, he has engaged more fully with people who reinforce his beliefs that he is a victim of the government and the president. His family situation has continued to suffer, as have his finances and his other close relationships.

Jason is more committed to being right about being a victim than accepting the help he is being offered to rectify his situation, getting employed and getting back on track again. His "family" has become the movement, and those he loved have been abandoned as a result of his rage.

The Devil's Food WordFood Diet is the most extreme of all the diets. People on this diet are opinionated beyond all reason. Their views are "my way or the highway." They repeatedly (and loudly) reiterate their pet theories, and deny all facts to the contrary. People on a Devil's Food Diet are the conspiracy theorists, those in rigid politics, religion; the isms spewing their judgmental view of the world in black and white. They have an us-versus-them attitude. "You're either with me or against me." They are obsessive. People who draw from the Devil's Food Diet need to be right even when they are dead wrong, dogmatic, argumentative, belligerent, fanatical and narrow-minded. To disagree is to invite acute disapproval or violence.

People develop these beliefs when they are very hungry for validation, or need others to corroborate their worldview. They can't tolerate any challenges to or questions about their viewpoints and in some extreme cases will kill to make their point.

In lesser cases this could be a boss who cannot tolerate any kind of insubordination or questioning. It might be a domineering father or mother who has to have complete control over members of their family. It could be someone who possesses a Napoleon complex who wields an unhealthy amount of power over others, to his or her own advantage, and others suffer for it.

In some cases, people like Jason have adopted an intense viewpoint because of a loss of some kind, or a change in their lives. For example, someone who has healed himself of a heroin habit may adopt a particularly radical form of religion. He then believes that everyone else needs to adopt that same form of worship because it saved him from his habit. He has embraced this religion with the same fervor that he once embraced heroin. He cannot see what he has done; all he knows is that everyone else must do as he has done or else he was wrong about his choice of redemption, and that cannot be the case. He needs to be seen with compassion, not ridiculed.

In other cases, people have adopted a significant movement like abortion rights or the anti-nuclear movement not so much because this appeals to them directly but because something in their personal lives has failed. These powerful anger-driven movements give them a legitimate voice and often positions of leadership. They also find fellowship and camaraderie in the cause with others of similar views. To remove them from this movement would take them away from the one place where they have been able to express their frustration and force them to address the issues in their lives that really need to be handled. Besides, they have an army of friends who back up their views and who follow them. That is hard to relinquish when one has become personally identified with a large movement.

You might hear these kinds of phrases:

> "The government is out to get us."

> "If you don't believe this way, you're going to hell."

> "I make the rules in this house."

> "You don't like it, you can leave."

> "I'm your husband and you will do what I tell you to do."

> "I don't care what they told you in that class. In my shop, we do it my way."

> "Your feelings don't matter to me. I'm the boss."

> "I am the way to heaven and you must follow me or die."

> "Open your mouth again and I'll beat the s__t out of you and your mother."

Body language for the Devil's Food Diet can include aggressive posturing, getting into people's faces, staring others down, and showing great intensity in facial expressions. Their tone can be powerful and assertive, forceful and intense. They are totally focused when talking about their beliefs, perhaps starting out quietly, but if challenged, can escalate into argument. Eye contact is very intense and focused, often without a break. When engaged fully or challenged, they can escalate into shouting or screaming. At this point their eyes will be defocused, and it will be nearly impossible to reach them. They may get physical and forceful, even dangerous or threatening. They can also totally withdraw from the world into their own universe, and get violent when others try to reach out to them.

Their fears include:

> *I may be all alone in the world but I am backed by my Higher Power.*
>
> *I am an army of one in my beliefs.*
>
> *I have to enroll everyone to make myself right.*
>
> *You have to join me or you must be the enemy.*
>
> *I am in total control here.*
>
> *No one can contest me.*

The motivations behind this diet might be:

> *Everyone who doesn't support me is my enemy.*
>
> *I have to be right.*
>
> *I will destroy anything/anybody in order to be right.*
>
> *I am the master of my universe.*

God (or a higher power) is on my side.

I'm in charge here; you have to obey me.

You have to support my beliefs.

Common negative responses from Devil's Food Diet:

"Stay away from them, they're freaks."

"I hate them, they're just animals in robes."

"You just don't understand the Bible. Let me tell you…"

"You should see things my way."

"You can't tell me what to do!"

"You guys are morons."

WHAT TO EXPECT FROM THIS WORDFOOD DIET

The Devil's Food Diet poses some special challenges. Here are some behaviors and suggestions for how to respond:

My Agenda Is Really Important: People on this diet engage you with real power and purpose. An appropriate response is to acknowledge their topic and move on. It doesn't serve to engage if you are not interested in it. You will not win the argument and it's very hard to extricate yourself once involved.

Strict Adherence to Their Point of View: They cannot be budged from their stance. A response would be to be open and accepting. Remember that in many cases the Devil's Food behaviors are fear based. This is a group that deserves patience and understanding, not anger and fear on our part. While you may not change them, they don't deserve hate and ridicule.

Rigidity, No Giving on the Topic: A response would be to validate their point of view as a way of thinking, then change the subject to a neutral one. You might exit the conversation gracefully by saying, "You know, you could be right." Especially in the arena of religious views, all bets are off. People have a right to their beliefs so long as others are not being hurt. You may not wish to be enrolled, so simply move on to another more neutral topic so you can have a discussion, if possible. Sometimes, however, you may have to walk away to get a little air. Devil's Food WordFood Diet conversations indicate that discussions are either win or lose, and they have to be right. Don't get caught up in this ugly battle.

Narrow Viewpoint: Value the viewpoint and then move on.

Fanatical Approach: When you are faced with fanaticism, the best way is to find your way around it. There is no reasoning with it, no arguing with it unless you are one yourself and you just love a good fight. Be gracious but be gone. There are times to leave well enough alone.

My Way or the Highway: A domineering boss or parent on the Devil's Food Diet is terribly fearful of losing his or her grip or losing the love of the family. To this person the only way to maintain it is to dictate. This is fear-based behavior, and one approach would be to reverse directions in the conversation. Try talking about something else and get him off that tack entirely. See what happens. See if he can relax a bit. Otherwise, ensure he will get what he needs and soothe the part of him that needs compliance.

I'm Here to Enroll You in My Cause: An appropriate response is don't drink the Kool-Aid. Your role here is to understand where your boundaries lie. You have nothing to prove and you don't have to argue your cause. People on the Devil's Food Diet will not hear you anyway. They only have ears for their side of the story. And they are determined to get you in their camp. Be gentle about drawing a line in the sand for what makes you comfortable about conversations at the office, at church, in your community. You may have to cut off contact completely. But do so without anger. Remember to take the higher road and understand where they are coming from. It's not about you. It's about letting them walk their own path, and that path needs to go by you, not through you.

POSITIVE RESPONSE: HEALTHY WORDFOOD FOR A HEALTHY DIET

Even though this will seem counterintuitive, what's needed is HeartBreads of compassion; love and understanding of the journey that this challenging group is on. When you are engaged in conversations with people on this diet, you will need to use plenty of HeartBreads patience, and you will be doing the listening a lot. Try to understand their need to be heard, offer them that listening ear and value their viewpoint.

Use Energy Enhancers to offer gentle acknowledgment of their viewpoint. Don't get caught up in the emotionality and passion, but hold up a mirror to them. Character Fiber will allow you to set boundaries and be clear about what you need to do, whether it's to say, "Thanks, but no thanks" or "Please, let's not discuss this again."

APPEAL TO THE HIGHER GOOD

George has already tried to help Jason on a functional level with his resume and been refused. It may be time for him to try another tactic and appeal to Jason's sense of duty as a father and a husband. He can use HeartBreads, Energy Enhancers, Character Fiber, and Balance Builders to reach across the divide that has developed between them.

> *"Jason, you've always been a great provider for your family. They need you now more than ever. Don't let them down."*
>
> *"Jason, your family is counting on you to provide for them. You're bigger than a bad patch. Let's see how we can get through this as a family, together."*
>
> *"Jason, I know you love your family and they love you. They need you right now. You've got the brains to get through this. What resources do you need?"*
>
> *"You've always been a winner and I've always looked up to you. Let's find that part of you again. What's it going to take to get back on your feet?"*
>
> *"Jason, I respect what you believe, but your family needs you now. Let's put our beliefs aside and take care of business. How do we get started together?"*

Devil's Food	Response
My Agenda Is Really Important	Acknowledge…and move on.
Strict Adherence	Be open and accepting, then move on.
Rigidity	Validate point of view as a way of thinking, and change subject.
Narrow Viewpoint	Value the viewpoint, then move on.
Fanatic Approach	Go around the topic.
My Way or the Highway	Reverse directions in the conversation.
I'm Here to Enroll You in My Cause	Don't drink the Kool-Aid.

Food for Thought

"You know, you may be right." According to conflict resolution expert Stephanie Roth, this phrase has a way of defusing conflict. It can come in very handy when dealing with people on a Devil's Food Diet. Even when you feel that the person you're talking to is dead wrong, this saying is a good way of getting around, and out of, the conversation. This expression works wonders when it's more practical to withdraw rather than to argue the point and be right. Remember, people on this diet have to be right—at all costs. You can't win this argument. It's best to concede and recede.

When dealing with other diets, you can use the phrase as a way to derail an argument as in, "You may be right. Let's research this and figure it out." Or, "You might be right. Did you see that article in the *New York Times* that refuted that claim?" Remember, some people would rather be right than be happy, as my friend Orvel Ray likes to say. And he's right.

Above all, this group requires some of our greatest compassion. People on the Devil's Food Diet are often experiencing considerable pain. They are subject to ridicule, hatred and misunderstanding. They may be ethnic groups, religious sects, or bosses who are being edged out of their positions. They may be parents or family members who were severely abused in their childhoods and this is their coping mechanism. They may be bitter, vicious, pissed off, criminal, hateful and destructive. Or they may be genuinely evil human beings. As poor as it may be, it is the best they can do with the tools they have in their tool box.

It takes courage on our part to offer kindness, warmth, love and forgiveness to a group that can be damning, angry, even willing to kill for its beliefs. It's easy to simply condemn them. But they are just people, and it is their humanity that calls to us for understanding even though on the surface they may not receive it. It is up to us to feed them the healthiest WordFood available and invite them to dine on a healthy diet. It is their choice to partake.

In any case, where it is clear you can't make any headway and there is imminent danger, remove yourself and your loved ones immediately. There are some people who will not be reached with Word-Food of any kind. Stop talking and start walking away. Fast.

Food for Thought

If you have ever been caught up in the excitement of a movement and been convinced of the rightness of what you are doing, you can understand the extreme passion that people on a Devil's Food Diet can have for their agenda. You may be involved in a group that instills this kind of passion in you now. All that is necessary to help here is to have empathy, and to not judge harshly. However, if you have a loved one caught in the net of a movement where you feel they are endangered, get professional help involved. You most likely don't have the skills to extricate someone from an organization yourself. They must have the desire to get out. There are legal and ethical issues involved, not just your emotional ones.

As for domineering bosses and spouses, sometimes the only way to heal the issue is to remove yourself from it entirely. This may mean you reach out for support through this process. These are not people who are likely to change. Protect yourself first or you may find that you are poisoned by their toxic words.

BALANCED DIET

Ted and Julia have been close friends for seven years. They trust each other's opinions, work together on projects and spend personal time together. While they sometimes disagree, they value each other's opinions and look to each other for guidance and insight. When there is a disagreement, it is handled with respect. They don't take each other for granted. Ted and Julia take real pleasure in each other's company, whether it's to see a movie or to create documents for work. They are not afraid to give each other feedback on behavior that isn't up to the standards they have come to expect from each other, for they want each other to succeed. They regularly express their love and regard for each other.

People who are on this healthy Balanced WordFood Diet engage each other with regard, respect and care. This is the most vibrant of all the WordFood Diets and the one that sets the example for all the others. People who are on the Balanced Diet serve others rich WordFood meals of courtesy, honesty, grace and thoughtful listening. They draw appropriately from the WordFood Pyramid to speak to people in their lives in the best possible ways. Their relationships are built on trust and mutual regard. Their intention is to keep their communications open and respectful. What are missing are personal agendas, secrets, issues and resentment.

Mark Twain once said, "I can live for two months on a good compliment." That's how powerful affirming words can be to us, says Gary Chapman, in *The Five Love Languages: How to Express Heartfelt Commitment to Your Mate*, Northfield Publishing, 1995. Chapman writes that affirming words constitute one of the critical Five Love Languages that we use to express each other's value.

People engage in the Balanced Diet when they have learned to trust each other's intentions. They care about each other's welfare. Married couples, for example, who have come through challenging times but who have learned to trust each other to make the marriage work, to love each other no matter what, to be kind to each other no matter what their mood may be, are on a Balanced Diet. A boss who treats each employee with respect and regard no matter her mood, no matter the pressure she may be feeling is on a Balanced Diet. She makes time for her employees' issues and problems, has room for them in her schedule any time they need her ear and she ensures they get credit for their accomplishments. Chances are she gets top performance from her team.

People on the Balanced WordFood diet are extraordinary listeners. They listen with their whole person when they are talking. They watch your eyes, facial expressions, body language and mood. As they talk they are watching for the impact of their words on you so, if they need to, they can adjust what they say, their mood, tone or word choice. When they are listening and talking, they are completely receptive. It's not all about getting their point across so much as creating an environment of engagement. There is stillness between them that is safe, where they feel good about making their points. They listen with the intent to fully understand. They aren't just waiting for you to finish to make their point; they want to know your ideas, thoughts and feelings.

Balanced Diet phrases sound like:

> *"Thanks very much for hearing me out."*
>
> *"You're a great boss. I appreciate working for you."*
>
> *"You can count on me. I have your back on this project."*
>
> *"I treasure the time we've had to spend together."*
>
> *"You've got great kids. They've been a pleasure to have with us this weekend."*

"You're a trusted friend, and I will always be here for you."

"I believe in you; you're going to get through this with flying colors!"

"You're beautiful in my eyes and that's all that matters."

People who use the Balanced WordFood Diet let others know where they stand. They are quick to compliment, to show warmth and be consistently gracious. You can count on kind words and support from this group. You can also trust that you will get coaching when you need it. You receive honest feedback that keeps you whole instead of full of holes. Because of the high level of trust, a boss who draws from the Balanced Diet provides a performance review that has no surprises. For the times that you may go off course with someone on the Balanced WordFood Diet, it's easier to get back on course. The fundamental motivation is to be clear, conscious and open. They tend to be very patient with other's issues and work with their process and where they are rather than use force.

People on this diet can be very charismatic, when charisma is redefined as "how people feel about themselves when they walk away from you." When you feel valued, heard and graced, that's charisma. People on this diet are focused on *you*, on ensuring you feel heard and valued. That is true magnetism. Anyone who develops the skills of the Balanced WordFood Diet can be captivating because it is so much about giving and service.

People who are on this diet are vulnerable in the most positive sense of the word. Open to what they see and feel from others, they are totally receptive to what others bring to the relationship. They are available to hearing and experiencing. They do so without judgment. These people want to understand whom they are with. Their defenses are down and you feel as though you can connect immediately.

The body language that you will see in this diet is open, warm and inviting. There is likely to be touching, within the boundaries of the relationship and accepted office rules. Expect hugging as well. The Balanced WordFood diet has what Lee Glickman, in *Be Heard Now*, Broadway Books, 1999, calls "soft eyes," which are convivial and friendly. You're met with openness and graciousness, with a welcoming face. They keep their eyes on yours (with exceptions in certain cultures) and hold your attention. They ensure that you know you're being heard through attentive body posture and eye contact, leaning forward and expressing sounds of affirmation. They may touch you while listening to you to keep the connection strong. They express pleasure in your company by their facial expressions and physical presence. Depending on the gender and culture, there may be greater or lesser physical closeness involved, but invariably people on the Balanced WordFood Diet work to make you feel comfortable in their presence, appreciated and acknowledged through verbal and nonverbal signals.

There are no fears behind this diet. People on the Balanced Word-Food Diet operate out of respect for themselves first, and because of this, offer this respect for others. They have regard for other's boundaries and feelings. They understand the importance of community. When two people need to have a conversation about challenging behaviors, it can be done without the typical concern of being shamed or hurt. Both understand that the other's intentions are good and true and a larger need is being served.

The motivation that drives the Balanced Diet is to create the best good for everyone involved. Clear, open, honest communication, valued partnerships and genuineness are hallmarks of this diet. It is defined by its courtesy and graciousness.

WHAT TO EXPECT FROM THIS DIET

Some of the behaviors you can expect from the Balanced Word-Food Diet are listed along with the appropriate response, which is to give the same in return.

Principled, Truthful Communication: The parties are open, respectful and honest.

Balanced Communication and an Active Give and Take on Both Sides: Both parties are open and participating at a high level of openness; there is an easy exchange between the two. Because the exchanges are based on collaboration there is no hoarding of information or resources.

Appropriate Boundaries Are Respected: Both parties are aware of and careful of personal and professional boundaries. There is no jockeying for power, influence or resources.

Honest Feedback Both Ways: Both parties are able to provide feedback personally and professionally and it is both given and received openly and with trust that the intentions are true. There is no fear that someone is going to come away hurt or damaged.

A CARING EXCHANGE

In Ted and Julia's working and personal relationship, they are appreciative and respectful. They also support each other's growth so there is mutual development. They remind each other of their importance to each other. Their relationship is marked by Heartbreads, Energy Enhancers and Character Builders.

"Julia, you are really special to me."

"Julia, the birthday gift you gave me was the nicest I have ever gotten."

"Julia, I appreciate your taking the time to bring over the extra books. Thank you."

"I know you will win that project. You've got the talent and skills to get the contract."

Julia gets regular insights from Ted and he helps her out with work projects.

"Ted, the graphics on this website are beautiful."

"You are one of the wisest people I know."

"Thanks for working extra hard on this project for me."

"You are going to get through this. I completely believe in you."

Balanced Response

Balanced	Response
Balanced Communication, Give & Take	Both parties work to create open conversation.
Honest Feedback Both Ways	Both parties keep the reactions and responses flowing.
No Fear-Based Behavior	There is courage in communication.
Principled Communication	High standards of messaging.
Appropriate Boundaries Are Respected	All parties honor the needs of others.
Warm and Caring Interactions Create Value	Intimacy is formed through relationships.

Food for Thought

Lee Glickstein in his book, *Be Heard Now!* talks about the importance of connecting with an audience before starting to speak. He says that it's key to have a moment of silence to let the audience connect with you, to feel you, to see you and to take you in. He says that the use of the pause is a key part of a powerful presentation, because the audience can take a breath and think about your salient points.

This works in conversations, as well. Especially when you want to express something that's very important, emotional or difficult. It's important to be still. Be available. For a few moments, consciously create a space where you are completely present so that your conversational partner can be with you to connect. Instead of rushing into the topic at hand, give yourselves time to be with each other and establish a heartfelt bond. This creates trust and the essential connection that allows the information to be better received.

Whether you are talking to your spouse, your teenager, a difficult employee, a loved one or a boss, it is vital that you create this critical bond before you begin. Take a deep breath and allow yourself just a few seconds to look the person in the eyes with a soft expression. Keep your face open and welcoming. Then move into the topic you need to discuss. If it is a difficult conversation, you can then better deal with the responses because you first made that connection. You took the person into account instead of treating him or her like a chore to be handled. Glickstein says that, "People would rather hear the truth than anything else we can tell them." It is best to do it with courtesy, kindness and connection.

The purpose of this book is to develop your skills so that your interactions create a primarily Balanced WordFood Diet, and that you are regularly drawing from each of the four groups of the WordFood Pyramid every day and in all your relationships. As you develop your skills, you will find it easier to dip into the

HeartBreads for graciousness and care, honesty and love, warmth and listening skills. You will find that the Energy Enhancers come more easily as you remember to acknowledge yourself for your own everyday accomplishments. You will look for ways to develop Character Fiber to mentor and coach people in your world. You will have enlisted a coach or two in your own life, having realized you deserve to be developed to a higher level of performance, just like top athletes. And you will be willing to use Balance Builders to bring people back on track, or be sure that a high performing employee gets recognition. You know that both sides of that behavior need attention. And that you're the one who should take the step.

You develop skills in the Balanced WordFood Diet through practice by using the WordFood Pyramid Groups every day. Daily use strengthens you. Feeding yourself these important Food Groups is essential because it's your primary responsibility to keep yourself healthy. Greet yourself with warmth, love and respect in the morning, and carry yourself out the door with courage and enthusiasm. You know that you have resources to deal with the diets that you have to face every day. The more you feed others these wonderful foods, the more likely you will heal them, and get the Balanced WordFood Diet back in return.

WHEN YOU SLIP

Even the most dedicated Balanced Diet person will sometimes get angry, or function out of one of the other diets. It's a natural part of life, responding to its everyday ups and downs. When you are faced with people who are presenting you with any of the other diets in this book, even if you intend to do your best, on a bad day you are likely to respond in kind. Don't panic or get down on yourself. No matter how hard you try, you are likely to find yourself giving someone the cold shoulder one day, snapping at your kids or finding it hard to adjust to something new at work. Everyday stresses impact us and we can find ourselves responding to them by feeding ourselves and others unhealthy diets despite our best intentions.

What's important is to be conscious of what you are doing. Don't get angry, get aware. Awareness allows us to make better choices about our behavior, and to step back and choose a healthier diet. When you find yourself feeding people a Starvation WordFood Diet, for example, it's time to ask yourself what or who is hurting you, and how can you heal this in yourself. How can you take responsibility for fixing the problem? If your behavior is impacting others in a negative way, what are you willing to do to start feeding people healthy WordFood again? It all starts with how you are talking to yourself.

When you find yourself feeding others a Ballpark WordFood Diet because you have similar fanatics at the office, are you willing to take stock in the behavior and change the example you're setting? Can you step back and become aware of what you're doing and redirect your energy? Instead of being swept away by the emotions of the moment, this is a huge opportunity for growth.

Food for Thought

Sometimes when you think you are doing a good job listening, you aren't. Watch where your mind is going. When you're with someone, do your eyes wander the room or do they stay focused on your conversational partner? Are you listening to understand or are you waiting for them to finish so that you can make your point—or your getaway? Are you impatient? Do you feel the need to get on with the discussion, that they are wasting your time? All these are characteristics of selfishness and self-importance. You don't really care about the other person. You're just marking time—barely—waiting to get on with your own life.

The same thing is true for when you're on the phone. You know when someone is typing on their computer when you're talking to them. In fact you probably know the precise moment their attention moves away. Suddenly you're getting mmm-hmmm's instead of real words. This is incredibly inconsiderate.

Remember how this feels next time you're tempted to multitask when you're on the phone with a client or someone who needs to connect. It's time to take a deep breath and slow down. Be present for this person. You don't know what you are missing. How would you feel if you needed someone to hear you and they were fidgeting, looking elsewhere, obviously itching to go? Or they were busy typing or checking emails when you needed their full attention? You'd be hurt, or at least offended, by their rudeness. We show up in this world to be here for each other. There is a lesson in learning to slow down. Whatever else is going on in your life can wait five minutes while you attend to another person. If not possible, make another date to talk in depth. You will be glad you did, and so will they. This is WordFood at work.

Every moment of every day you'll find an opportunity to become more aware and to make a change in what you are doing. It is possible to be asleep and be carried along by our emotions. But it is also possible to wake up to what you are doing, and make a healthier choice about your actions. You can change what you are saying to yourself and to others and in that moment change the situation. This does take courage, but it is what builds character and personal power. These are the kinds of everyday choices that make us into the kind of people others respect and look up to as mentors and leaders.

BANKRUPTCY TO BIG BREAK

October 1997, Spokane, Washington. My husband and I were heavily in debt, with a house, a couple of cars, some land in Idaho and a lot of hope that we could somehow turn it all around and find jobs in this northwestern hamlet. I was also ill with migraines, averaging nearly twenty of them a month. We had left the mortgage behind in North Carolina where I'd been laid off, and headed West.

In short order, we filed for bankruptcy, and then for divorce. My business collapsed and so did my credit rating. I lost my land, my house, and my car was repossessed. My teeth started falling out. A hysterectomy followed and so did my fifteenth breast surgery. My dog got killed in front of my house and my second dog died in my arms. I was in two car wrecks; the second damaged my left knee. As a disabled veteran, I was living on minimal support from the federal government, dealing with these migraines nearly every day.

Still, desperate to find work, I sent out more than four hundred resumes. These generated one interview with a large company, but I didn't get the job. I wouldn't have been able to work anyway due to the headaches. Suicide was a constant thought. I nearly acted on that impulse several times. I was feeding myself terribly toxic WordFood every day, all day long.

In the midst of all this, I was networking, all over town. And I was meeting all kinds of women, powerful women who didn't know each other. I began putting a couple of these women together in a small group on Thursdays once a month, then a few more. Soon this group—we named them the Great Broads— took off. I hunted for the smartest, most talented, highest level women—women of every color and culture—I could find, and these women fed off each other's talent and smarts. They were lonely and needed each other. I was able to be the glue that created those relationships.

When I brought them in I fed them a steady diet of supportive WordFood about their skills and talents. I introduced them to the group using Energy Enhancers. For our younger members we used Character Fiber to help them find incredible new jobs and launch new careers. At the time, we didn't have the WordFood model to describe what we were doing, but in effect that's what it was.

I wrote about these women and published articles locally, promoting them and their businesses. This effort helped their businesses grow through introductions.

None of them were aware of the challenges I was facing until one day one of them pulled me aside and probed. She saw the stress in my face. Word got around the group and by Christmas, the group surprised me with a brand new computer, which hooked me up to the Internet for the first time. It was a gift of massive proportion. Then they helped me find legal help to file for full disability, which transformed my financial situation.

This group pulled together and helped lift me up by the bootstraps. They taught me that when you are in extremity, you bestow. The more you give, the less you are preoccupied by your own circumstances. You can experience your value by making a difference in other's lives. They also taught me how to receive love. These women got me through the toughest time of my life. What became The Hubbel Group (see *Networking Magic,* by Jill Lublin and Rick Frishman) became an amazing organization that supported, nurtured and launched several successful careers.

While The Hubbel Group ultimately broke ranks after I left Spokane to deal with a dying mother in 2000, many of us are still in touch. The experience changed us all. It taught me how women and people of color networked differently. It gave me a big break, a new business and a new life. After I got back to Colorado, The Hubbel Group Inc. was born. The Hubbel Group of Spokane was the author of that new venture. I thank every single one of those amazing, wonderful women.

To sum it up, we had been feeding each other a steady Balanced WordFood Diet, and we grew and prospered on that rich fodder. We uplifted each other, supported each other and believed in each other. That's what nourishing WordFood can do.

WORDFOOD MAGIC

One way that my good friend and mentor, Orvel Ray Wilson, CSP trains salespeople how to create a strong connection with the customer is by taking words from the person's own sentences and reusing them in their questions. He calls this technique "Their-a-Phrasing" (as opposed to "paraphrasing").

Recently Orvel Ray and I were discussing a trip I had taken to New Orleans.

"So you were in New Orleans. Did you get to Preservation Hall?"

"No, But we did go out to eat."

"Where did you go out to eat?"

"The Red Fish Grill."

"The Red Fish Grill? What kind of fish do they serve?"

"Red fish!"

"So what did you have?"

"I had the red fish with fried scallops."

"How were the scallops?"

"Oh my gosh! They were huge! They were fat, juicy, wonderful…"

I was instantly transported back to the restaurant, the delicious scallops rolling on my tongue. My face was pink and happy, I was smiling, and the memory was immediate and real. Orvel Ray had succeeded in taking me right back to the Red Fish Grill and the very moment that I had bitten into that first scallop, and I could literally see them on my plate. As I was telling him about the scallops I was excited, and waving my hands in the air, tickled about this delicious meal.

If you notice in the dialogue, each question that Orvel Ray asked was formed around a *key word or phrase* taken from my previous answer. That sparked the next question and the next answer. It demonstrated he was listening, and it encouraged me to give him more detail about my experience and my story; I wanted him to hear all about it. The more he queried me, the more detail I began to recall until the Red Fish Grill swam into view, the dishes appeared on the table, and suddenly there were those amazing scallops. I felt that he genuinely wanted to know about my meal, and I was eager to share the experience.

DEALING WITH THE WORDFOOD DIET ARCHETYPES

One of the challenges of dealing with the archetypes is your own ego. It's easy to get frustrated, angry and offended by the behaviors of other people. They *can* be annoying. The words they say *can* hurt. Their anger can be directed at *you* and it's easy to take things personally. Yet, here is an opportunity to rise above your natural reactions and make a very brave choice to see and feel differently.

Let's say that you have been dealing with someone on a Meat & Potatoes WordFood Diet who has decided to let go of all his anger about changes going on at the company. You've been able to establish his trust, but now he's decided to take out all that frustration on you. This isn't what you asked for, but it's what you get. Your options are:

> *Strike back and say it wasn't your fault that things went badly for him.*
>
> *Sit in angry silence until he's done.*
>
> *Leave. After all, it's his pity party.*
>
> *Have the courage to bear witness to his anger and pain.*

By choosing this last option you are helping him keep his dignity. Let him work this out in your presence, listen and let him vent.

Recognize that it has nothing to do with you, and that your presence is a much needed gift to him. When he is done, ask what you both need to do next. This allows him to take the next step responsibly. It's remarkable how often just the process of letting loose does much of the healing.

This is true for many of the diets where there are powerful fears lurking behind the dysfunctional behaviors. You may have been the one who initiated that person's anger in the first place. Then he built up greater rage in his isolation. When he finally opened up, you are ambushed with complaints about grievances you didn't commit. It takes real courage to not respond in kind. It takes courage to let the fury blow by you. The truth is that the vehemence has nothing to do with you and never did. Can you stand in the face of this and be the kind of friend this person truly needs? Once the onslaught is over he is likely to feel bad for abusing you. Instead of being angry or self-righteous, offer your understanding of his condition. Let him regain his dignity. Here is a chance to grow beyond who you have ever been before. You can become another person. This is virtue. And it is also friendship. It will not be forgotten.

Consider how you might feel if you were in the same situation. How would it feel if someone stood his ground with you while you vented? Now think about how would it be if he offered his kind understanding, without judgment? Allowed you to save face? Chances are you'd be a combination of embarrassed and grateful. If this person handled this situation with grace, you would both walk away whole.

This also means that you don't gossip about this episode throughout the company or to your family. Preserving dignity means what happens between you and this person stays between you. That is a sacred trust.

CHAPTER SIX

WordFood Spices and JunkFood

WORDFOOD SPICES

All good chefs have at their command a fully stocked kitchen of options, and so do you. Let's take a look at the provisions you may need along the way as you serve up sustenance for the diets around you.

Sweet Spices

The spice cabinet is full of words that you can use to energize your conversation. These words add aroma, color and gusto to our conversations. Like everything from salt and pepper to chilies and cilantro, we use adjectives and adverbs to make our language come alive.

Whether you're writing or speaking, the spice cabinet is as broad and wide as the English language is varied. The best way to bring spice into your world is to read books. Buy or rent books by the great authors. Listen to books on tape as you drive and let the beauty of our magnificent language grace your ears and tickle your thought processes. Challenge yourself to add new and delightful words to your vocabulary every day. Let the word "spin" become "pirouette," let "cold" become "arctic." Find ways to expand your repertoire and become artful in your WordFood kitchen.

Spicy Words:

merchant	dubious	tenacious
nuisance	jubilant	announced
bedazzled	adept	monstrous
pungent	remnant	lascivious
perplexed	profound	fickle
putrid	baffled	notch
catawampus	omniscient	discombobulated
exploding	savor	delectable
despondent	grim	atrocious
malicious	divulge	anxious
elaborate	stupendous	ostentatious
plausible	farfetched	absurd
anguish	ennui	comfortably
meld	frolicsome	ennui
loquacious	manifold	boisterous
annex	diligent	cunning
manifold	bogey	frigid
crotchety	fathom	hollow
innovative	facetious	nimble
skeptical	quail	insidious
embellish	dialect	fetid
procrastinate	solitude	commute
travesty	motivate	contentious
guileful	infuriated	persist
apoplectic	verbose	appall
trivial	felicitous	ambiguous
lavishly	anomaly	feeble

—www.SpicyWordoftheWeek.com

Spicy sayings for loved ones

The spices of affectionate words are sweet like cinnamon and nut-meg. Sometimes they waft through the air and touch the heart like hot chocolate on a winter's day. So many people in your life are hungry for words of love. Fill your cabinets with sweet spices, add some hot ones, and notice how they constantly replenish themselves with use. You can never run out because they come from love. Icing is also found in this part of the cabinet, as well as the maraschino cherries for the top of the banana split. Go ahead, why not?

These are the words that our loved ones live for, the words that candy coat us as they come through us, that grace our tongue as we use them. WordFood sweet spices are the living words of love and affection that are so often left to gather dust in the cupboard as our families go hungry for treats. Open this cabinet more often and treat those in your broad circle to your words of warmth, acknowledgment, affection and regard. But remember, a touch of sugar goes a very long way.

Words like this include:

> *"You are the cream in my coffee."*

> *"I hate getting out of bed with you still in it."*

> *"You make me want to cuddle all day."*

> *"You're the magic that puts the sparkle in my life."*

> *"I can't wait to wrap my arms around you when I see you again."*

Hot Spices

This is the hot stuff of WordFood, big adjectives that are used to impress. Used sparingly, these WordFood Hot Spices are added to make our stories and points bigger, better, more awe-inspiring. Just like you might use Tabasco sauce on scrambled eggs, or add jalapenos to your bowl of chili, this is fine for taste.

> *"Your eyes sparkled like sapphires in the candlelight."*

> *"The thunderclouds boiled furiously overhead as though they were being stirred by a giant spoon."*

But anything that is used to excess tends to numb the tongue, and the ear. Too many peppers or too much Tabasco sauce and you've overwhelmed the meal. Too many adjectives and you've numbed your listener. You can no longer differentiate when everything you talk about is "awesome," "incredible," "stupendous," or "amazing!"

When you choose sweet or hot WordFood spices, decide what point are you trying to make. What needs to be said, and what kind of language best serves you? You'll find that a few well-placed splashes of sauce or sweet spices will get your point across quite nicely. Like the Boy Who Cried Wolf, when you get known for constant exaggeration, no one will take you seriously. Save your chilies for when it's really deserved or everything will sound the same.

Sample sentences where the jalapenos have gone wild:

> *"It is going to take a bazillion years to get through medical school."*

> *"I ate the whole cow."*

> *"He's 900 years old."*

> *"I am so hungry I could eat a horse."*

"There are millions of other things to do."

"You could be Miss Universe."

"It took light years for this to work."

—From Poetry, Hyperbole and Superlatives, Wikipedia

OTHER CONDIMENTS

The kitchen also holds many other WordFood Diet goodies that we can use in everyday conversations. In our talks using Character Fiber, and especially Balance Builders, it's helpful to use words that help digest that heavy information. Like tuna salad, which is best served with mayonnaise, the WordFood refrigerator door holds an assortment of condiments and spreads.

Some "mayonnaise" phrases are:

"I know you will do this well."

"You have the fortitude to take this on."

"You just need to believe in yourself."

"You are terrific at this. You're just a little off course."

"You've got the skills to get this done."

"You have great courage."

"Thank you for hearing me out."

WORDFOOD JUNKFOOD

Junk food is usually stashed in the pantry, where we periodically go to binge. Rather than a supply of potato chips, cookies and other empty calories, however, WordFood JunkFood consists of conversations with people who take up our time but don't add value to our lives. These are people who can suck the energy out of our day, who whine, complain, argue, or otherwise take advantage of our friendship. When you think about it, they don't bring joy or enlightenment. They are energy depleters. We care about them, but they drag us down.

JunkFood empty calories sound like:

> "My back hurts so bad. I'm always hurting. My doctor says that I have to have…"

> "Aunt Charlotte told me that you wouldn't talk to her. You always call Susan but not her. You really should."

> "Why don't you ever go to dinner with the Everlys? They're nice people, too, you know."

> "That dog barks all day. It's so annoying. I don't know how you can stand it. Barking all the time. I'd call the police if I were you."

JunkFood could also be negative radio or television programming that brings us down. It could be messages from any source that doesn't provide us with hope or a positive way of thinking about ourselves and life. These WordFood calories add weight to us without adding life-enhancing energy, which keeps us alive and awake. Just as it's a good idea to sometimes clean out the pantry to get rid of the JunkFood so that we aren't tempted to eat it, it's a good idea to end negative friendships. If these are family members, try to set boundaries on the time you spend or how you allow these negative messages to affect you. It's also a good idea to turn off programming like television or music that doesn't serve your soul.

Sometimes this JunkFood can sound like:

Religious programs that demand money from vulnerable populations

Hate-based programming

Programming that has no informational, educational or arts value whatsoever

Soap operas

Gossip is also JunkFood, especially mean-spirited gossip. While it may be sweet, salty and delicious, it is dissatisfying and it rots our teeth and our souls. Participating in gossip is like eating candy with a foul filling that poisons us from the inside out. Over time the negative influence makes us resentful, hateful and envious of others. We're quick to make fun of others and can become bullies. If you're feeling low, vulnerable or unloved, you may be tempted to participate in office gossip or gossip among friends.

The tendency to spread rumors stems from other rank sources like bigotry and hatred, our arrogance and self-love, misogyny, misplaced anger and misinformation. We can spread venom about others when we are feeling threatened. Or we may strike out when we have been the subject of someone else's abuse or anger. It is very tempting to take our feelings of helplessness out on others by spreading viciousness. Don't! It may temporarily raise your spirits, but in the long run it will decay your humanity. Remove yourself from the source of this ugliness and find other ways to raise your dignity and self-worth that feel honorable. The giving back to others will be what makes you feel better about yourself. Gossip JunkFood often sounds like:

> "I heard that Anne is sleeping with Jonah. What did you hear?"

> "Word is that Bob's going to get laid off. Some said he was taking company funds."

> "Your best friend is cheating with Sue's husband."

> "Madge is a snitch and she tells on everyone in the office. You can't trust her."

> "Jeff got a raise and it's only because Susan thinks he's cute. He can't do anything right."

Conversations between 'teens and 'tweens are largely made up of this kind of discussion. They bully and harass by riffing on each other's faults and shortcomings. If you have children, one of the great gifts you can give them is the perspective that gossip is harmful and how it hurts *them* first. This may help them stop participating. At the very least it will start the discussion early, and put forth the question in their minds about how they would feel if they were the objects of the gossip. Teens' JunkFood is all about:

> "Did you see what Shana wore to school? OMG!"

> "He is such a dork!"

> "Nobody will ever go out with her."

> "Who does he think he is, popular? I don't think so!"

Another form of gossip comes from Hollywood. Entertainment magazines and pop culture television are full of worthless information about celebrities' private lives, which have nothing whatsoever to do with us. And it is pure JunkFood: reading it, talking about it, digesting it, giving time to it, whether it's the *National Enquirer* or the latest star gossip rag. There are those who are obsessed with this class of information while the days and weeks of their own lives tick by unlived and unloved. For example, can you answer these questions?

> *Why did Ellen DeGeneres quit American Idol only after one season?*
>
> *Which celebrity and dancer began dating after meeting on Dancing with the Stars?*
>
> *Who is supposed to be the father of Jen's baby bump?*
>
> *Who is Brangelina and are they pregnant again?*

If you know the answers to these questions, it may be time to find another source of reading material. Or, you may be spending too much time in checkout lines.

JunkFood is also wasted words and words that don't add value to the conversation, like constant repetition. When you catch yourself complaining or whining, you're feeding someone else JunkFood. JunkFood in this category is packaged in statements like:

> *"But I want it now."*
>
> *"Why can't I?"*
>
> *"Where's my (dinner, toy, phone, etc.)?"*
>
> *"What are you going to do for me?"*
>
> *"What have you done for me lately?"*
>
> *"Why not?"*
>
> *"But I did say please."*

"How come I didn't get one?"

"I want one like he got."

"It's not as nice as I wanted."

"You told me you'd get that for me."

"You said you'd take me if I wanted to go."

"You never let me have what I want!"

When an unsolvable issue is going around and around inside your mind and it isn't serving you, it's just driving you crazy—that's Junk-Food. Worrying about the future, driving yourself batty about things that may or may not happen are JunkFood. Mind space that is taken up with useless energy is JunkFood. Put your considerable brain power to work in the here and now, where it can serve you, not in the past where there is nothing to be done, or in the future where nothing has arrived yet. JunkFood in this context sounds like:

"Did I turn off the stove?"

"Did I remember to send that file?"

"Did I tell Jerry about the program dates?"

"What am I going to do when Allen gets here on the 20th?"

"How am I going to handle it when the will is distributed?"

"What if Saundra says yes when I ask her to marry me?"

"What if a hurricane hits the beach house in Florida next year?"

JunkFood is also not living in the present, when you spend your waking hours reliving the past or obsessing about the future. In fact, American culture teaches us to think this way. For example, during football season, you're not even minutes into the first quarter of a game before you're being harangued about the entertainment at halftime. Seconds into the second quarter you're hearing about the next game coming up. By half time you're hearing about the game that's being played Sunday night.

This is true for most television programming and the way we are taught to think—in the future, all the time. We are rarely in the here and now so that our minds are constantly filled with Junk-Food, the empty calories of material we can't digest. Americans tend to think about what's coming up tomorrow more than where they are right now so that the moment they are in is robbed. Add to this the use of technology, which further takes away from the experience of the moment at hand. People are existing but they in effect are somewhere else all the time, filling their minds with JunkFood. Is it any wonder we are dissatisfied with our lives? This kind of JunkFood is a constant reminder:

> *You are sitting in the car with your loved ones and all of you are on cell phones.*

> *You are in the living room with your loved ones and all of you are on some kind of technological device. Some of you are texting each other across the room.*

> *You can no longer have a quality conversation with your family members without involving a piece of equipment and distance of some kind.*

As for the quality of the programs you listen to, time is precious. Mind space is precious. Consider carefully what you want to put into your system. Sometimes it's fun to listen to a program that is pablum just as it's fun to eat a handful of potato chips, just not as a steady diet. Your body and your mind get flabby. That's why you have a 24/7 Garbage Filter (see next chapter). There is a plethora of podcasts, informational broadcasting, wonderful music and visually stimulating material that will feed your soul. Plan to occasionally indulge from the Pantry, but maintain a stimulating diet of WordFood and keep the JunkFood to a minimum.

CHAPTER SEVEN

WordFood Poisoning

TOXIC WORDS

There are evil people in the world, people whose intention is to do harm and leave behind a trail of disaster. Rarely is there anything one can do to deal with people like this when these behaviors are fully developed, unless you bring in a third party. This is especially true if you are dealing with spousal abuse or a dangerous situation at work (and have been dealt a Devil's Food Diet). In many cases you will need to first remove yourself from the situation for your own safety. You'll also need to decide whether to continue with the relationship after it has been through an intervention. In some cases it may not be possible.

Toxic Words sound like this:

> *"You worthless bitch. I should never have married you."*
>
> *"You'll never amount to anything."*
>
> *"I wish I'd never had you kids."*
>
> *"You're a worthless secretary. You can't do anything right."*

"I hate the sight of you. You are a filthy so and so."

"You are a waste of flesh. You should never have been born."

"You're stupid, you know that?"

"You're nothing but brats. Go to your room."

SLOW POISONING

In some cases Toxic WordFood Poisoning will be subtler, and get dished out over long periods of time. In this situation it's more insidious. Little comments are dropped here and there about your clothing, your appearance, your ideas, your personal value. This becomes a constant barrage of messages that serves to tear down your positive sense of self-worth and humanity. At the office, it could be a regular devaluing of your work, your importance to the team or to the company. In all cases, the end product is low self-esteem.

Sadly, within families, this can happen when parents take their own feelings of low self-esteem or anger out on their children. The children are abused, left to fend for themselves against a barrage of ugly Toxic WordFood for which they have neither antidote nor answer. Children are hurt the worst by these words, and are most likely to carry on the legacy if not healed by a healthy WordFood Diet of loving intervention.

RESPONDING TO WORDFOOD POISONING

It's very easy to respond in kind, in hate, with revenge to those who hurt us. It's easier to strike back at those who have evil in their hearts;

to those we perceive are out to get us. It's much harder to see those people as having once been tiny babies. There was a time when they were without malice, innocent, with the world in front of them. Something terrible must have happened to them for their behavior to have gone so awry. Or perhaps they were simply born broken. They are sociopaths—people without conscience. When they are being cruel to us, we are challenged to rise above the most basic of human emotions and offer the highest, to find the courage to offer love where it is most needed. This is a group that is severely damaged and in need of our help or at least our understanding.

When you are faced with someone who is vicious to you, the best response is to remove yourself from this person as quickly as possible, especially if there is potential physical violence involved. Sometimes it may take a while to realize that you're under this influence especially if it's been going on for a long time. You may be feeling bad about yourself and not know why. It can often take a lot of courage to remove yourself from an abusive situation because the other person often wields a great deal of psychological power. That's where intervention is important. In any case, your challenge is to create a warm and loving environment for yourself, because clearly you have not been feeding yourself a healthy WordFood diet. That's the most important step to take toward getting healthy.

In the table below are examples of Toxic WordFood Poisoning and its "antidote" of healthy WordFood. The unhealthy approaches to human interactions are on the left. They are the kinds of choices that people make when they come from fear, anger, hurt and disappointment. They lead to toxic responses, hurt, more fear, anger and negative behaviors. On the right are the opposite and healthy options that create openness, warmth, interaction, positive exchange, collaboration and high performance. They open the door to human potential and growth.

Toxic WordFood	Nutritious WordFood
(all about "me")	(all about "we")
Criticism	Coach
Condescend	Acknowledge
Avoidance	Actively engage
Silence	Conversation
Taking credit	Give credit
Discourage	Encourage
Put downs	Compliment
Microinequities	Equal treatment of all
Isms	Self-regulation and awareness
Disagreement	Agreement
Hostility	Warmth and graciousness
Punish	Catch them doing something right
Blame	Take responsibility
Find fault	Notice the best
Nitpick	Appreciate
Smother	Give space to breathe and succeed
Interrupt	Listen
Denial	Take responsibility
Threaten	Admire
Fear	Courage
Hate	Love
Viciousness	Kindness
Verbal abuse	Soothing words of acceptance
Mental abuse	Professional intervention

Food for Thought

When someone is feeling anger, he or she feels large and self-justified. However, that feeling is also isolating. It separates the person from others. Anger gives someone a feeling of being substantial and righteous. Anger has a sense of virtuousness about it, especially when it stems from a feeling of being mistreated. The more people feel wronged, the more they can build the argument and the greater their rage. However, rage only pushes others away—those who could otherwise offer help, love and understanding. This further increases the rage, the wrath of loneliness.

This becomes a self-reinforcing cycle. The more the person is angry, the more he rages, the more he pushes help away. Even in an angry mob, there is no cohesiveness among the members. Each is an island of insanity, many of whom, when asked, are unable to describe why they are so agitated.

This is why it is so important to offer understanding and compassion when faced with Toxic WordFood. You are faced with someone in trouble, who needs help. While that help may not always be accepted, be assured that some part of that person heard you. Above all, you took care of yourself. You didn't respond in kind and you didn't let the toxicity contaminate you. In some cases, the only response is to move away from the source. In others, you may be able to de-escalate the situation.

✳ ✳ ✳

CREATING A WORDFOOD GARBAGE FILTER

Every day you have choices on what you take in. These include your daily conversations, the programs you watch on television, the books on tape you listen to, radio and television programming, movies, what's on your iPod and much more. From this barrage of WordFood, you can choose to turn it off or just never expose yourself to it. You can change your circle of friends, get a new job, attend a different church, make many shifts in the kind of Word-Food you receive every day.

Ideally there should be a 24/7 WordFood "Garbage Filter" that protects you against harm. Your healthy self should always be defending you against negative input and messages that could damage your identity. This allows you to hear people's anger and know that it's not about you, that it's most likely about them. One of your great challenges in life is standing in the face of other people's fury and not taking it personally. In so many cases, anger is about something else entirely, and you happen to be present when it erupts. Or, if it is about you, the anger released is tinged with anger about many other things left unsaid, and you get the brunt of all of it and it is out of proportion. It takes courage and personal power to stand in front of another's negative behavior and realize you are not usually the source of it. Rather, if you can bear witness to it and just let it wash over you, you are doing great service. You simply need to feed yourself loving WordFood to stay whole in the face of such an onslaught.

Keep in mind that the most important WordFood you receive is what you say to yourself first thing in the morning. But the rest of the day is up to you. What are your choices?

1. Send it back to the "chef" with kindness

Let's say that someone says something to you that you find distasteful or hurtful. You want to handle the issue, and you choose to do so gracefully and responsibly. Here's an opportunity to put your good wisdom to work. You're going to send Toxic WordFood back to the chef. You can say:

> *"I'm sure you didn't mean to say it that way. What you probably meant was…"*
>
> *"I appreciate what you're trying to say here. Let me suggest…"*
>
> *"Thanks for your input. What I think you mean is …"*
>
> *"I understand that you are very angry. Let's find a way to deal with this situation so that you are satisfied."*
>
> *"Thank you for letting me know your feelings. How can we now work together?"*

What you're doing is sending some healing back with your rewording. No judgment, just sending it back and saying, "This isn't acceptable. Try again." You're laying down a boundary, which is critical in establishing your right to be you and not be abused by ugly WordFood.

2. Leave it on your "plate" and take it in

In this case you've received something you're happy to accept. You take in this meal and digest it in full, and it feeds you, heart and soul. Its contents provide sustenance for you and what you need to become in life. Embrace it! And mentally thank the person who offered it to you.

3. Spit it out

Let's say you were "fed" untrue information about yourself, that you took in and realized was harmful. Time to get rid of it. Spit that bad stuff out. Reword that Toxic WordFood and have an internal conversation that resets the bar where it belongs. You can always have your internal conversation so that you are fine with you. It's when you give others permission to feed you junk you're willing to digest, or lies about your value that you believe, that you get in trouble.

WORDFOOD THAT GIVES YOU "HEARTBURN"

What happens when you are given WordFood that tastes great going down but makes you sick later? This can be the case when you believe false promises by a salesperson or sweet lies from a dishonest lover. It can happen when you buy a product that doesn't perform up to par, or you believe a politician that lets you down. In all of these cases you made a conscious choice to take in the WordFood that was offered and digest it—and got sick on it later. You were let down, the product let you down, the person let you down, and the experience hurt.

Ultimately, there are no victims in life. You make a choice based on the best information available. You can be angry but the emotion hurts you, the one who feels the destructive emotion. Anger does nothing to salve the wound or bring things to right. The only choice is to accept and move on. Realize that in life there will be times you make conscious choices about taking in what's served you based on the best information possible. Later on you find out it was bad information. Getting angry now only makes you sicker and solves nothing. It makes the garbage pile even higher because you are poisoning yourself from your own kitchen. It's very hard to filter the garbage when it's coming from within, and your first responsibility is to feed yourself a healthy diet. Anger is poisonous.

In addition to anger, other Toxic WordFood that you may be feeding yourself includes:

Envy. Don't covet what you didn't get born with in this life. If you weren't gifted with long slim legs, don't waste your time burning with envy when a tall drink of water walks in. Enjoy your ample curves or celebrate your cerebral gifts instead.

Resentment. You can waste a lifetime resenting others for real and imagined hurts. Open the door to those discussions and put some sunshine on those hurts. Get them out in the open and clear the air.

Blame. This is a toxic way to keep from taking responsibility for your part in any situation. You are 100% responsible for your share. Buck up and see where you were part of the problem. Be the one to say I'm sorry first. Soothe the hurt and end the issue.

Shame. Don't let others heap shame on you. This toxic emotion takes years from you and makes you live in the shadows. It can leach love and life from us. Bring this out in conversations with trusted loved ones who can help. Speak up for yourself.

Bitterness. Life has rough spots. It's not all about you. We all have losses and hurts. Learn to find what is good about life and celebrate those things, and leave behind those losses or accept them as lessons. Bitterness is a canker that becomes a cancer, literally.

Self-hate. This emotion causes us to eat ourselves from the inside out, and to despise our vision in the mirror every day. Find one thing to admire, one aspect of yourself to respect. Just one new thing every day. Make it a habit. Soon you will find that there is a lot to like about yourself, and then it may move to self-admiration and eventually to love. Give it time.

Victim talk: When you're singing your "woe is me" song, you will lose a lot of friends, at least the quality ones. A few may hang around but these are the ones who want you in *their* pity party, as well. Life is too short to waste swimming in tears all the time. The best friends are those who want us to be truly happy, and they have no time for victims. Get over yourself. When you start up the "poor me," it's time to pour yourself a glass of wine and find something else to talk about!

These toxic internal conversations are WordFood choices that you will learn to turn off over time. They will start up and you can turn them off, change the channel. You will have learned a valuable lesson about what to take in next time you are faced with a similar meal.

Another form of WordFood poisoning is cynicism. Don't fall prey. The challenge is to stay open, engaged and curious about what life shows you, what people bring you. Let your experiences bring you discrimination, not defeat, to your heart.

A WORD ABOUT SOCIAL AND POLITICAL MOVEMENTS

You already know that you're responsible for your 24/7 Garbage Filter, when it comes to television and radio, the general media and other forms of input that you can turn off or on depending on what serves you. There are also movements that we alluded to in the Devil's Food Diet chapter, some of which can be very powerful and positive. But some can end with hurt or even death, as with the infamous Jonestown tragedy in November of 1978 when many people drank poisoned Kool-Aid because cult leader Jim Jones convinced them to.

Movements can be intensely compelling, especially at vulnerable times in our lives. This can happen when we have experienced a loss, a tragedy or are unhappy with the state of affairs of our nation. Or we might be empty nesters or just curious. Cleverly worded materials or convincing friends could be the way we get involved. The energy and enthusiasm of a committed group of people could be just what it takes to sweep us along into a movement that quickly takes up our savings, our homes, our investments, our life's work.

Other movements are nowhere nearly as dark. There are powerful movements for going green, saving wildlife, ending poverty and many others that mean you are leaving a legacy for good on the planet. These kinds of movements allow you to be surrounded by others who are focused on the positive side of making a difference, rather than being driven by anger or an anti-something movement. The energy involved in such a movement changes the conversation and draws a completely different circle of people. These are people who want to do the right thing by the community, to collaborate and find peaceful answers rather than to picket and fight. This is where you might find an excellent "home" to grow your own WordFood skills.

You also may find lots of pamphlets and materials, seminars and workshops that offer quick fixes to life's biggest problems. The New Age movement was one that offered solutions through crystals and channeling the words of dolphins and saints. Many people get caught up in these movements while losing sight of the simple fact that improving one's life takes hard work daily. It begins with the WordFood that you feed yourself. Change that conversation and everything else begins to change. The relationship you have with yourself is the single most important relationship you will ever have in your life.

There are other movements, too. People are committed to spiritual growth in churches, synagogues, all kinds of places of worship. You may find yourself drawn to a line of study that challenges you to rise above your level of thinking and emoting to a different kind of life. You may find yourself wanting to speak a wholly different kind of WordFood you can only find in this kind of environment where people wish to see themselves, and their world, differently. If you want to find it, it is surprising how quickly this kind of work finds you.

CHAPTER EIGHT

WordFood and Technology

Pick up the damned telephone and talk to someone.

Here's a question for you. How many emails are being sent out every day?

Answer: the number of emails sent per day in 2009 is estimated to be 247 billion.

–Radicati Group, 2009

Two hundred forty-seven billion messages per day means more than 2.8 million emails are sent every second. Around 80% of these millions of messages are nothing but SPAM and viruses.

The genuine emails are sent by around 1.4 billion email users.

These numbers are growing every day, meaning that not only are you getting plenty of general information in your mailbox daily, you are also getting a lot more junk. Eighty percent of what you get is pure crap, unless you consider all the jokes and snarky gossip sent you as great WordFood.

Some of this we let through our WordFood Garbage Filter and allow it to influence our thinking and our being. And some of it we probably shouldn't, when we consider what a waste of time it can be and how it affects us. That's what that Garbage Filter is for: to instantly discard what doesn't serve or support our best selves.

So what about this whole question of emails and tweets? As someone who was a relative latecomer to email, I enjoy its swiftness and convenience. But as with any other communication system, email breaks down. Messages get stuck in SPAM files, they don't arrive, people don't read them or, like any piece of paper, they get set aside to be read later. Because my system tells me when an email is read, I know that sometimes an email isn't touched for months. In some ways they are a convenience but, over time, I've also come to see emails as an excuse, as a reason not to pick up the damn telephone and call someone.

I can recall not long ago when my boyfriend at the time and I would get on the phone for four hours at a stretch and talk about... anything. Everything. Ideas. Concepts. Religion. Politics. I loved hearing his voice and he loved hearing mine. Yes, we had email but we loved being connected. We were on the phone so much because we lived six hours apart. When we were together we also talked for hours. Interestingly, after we broke up, we maintained our friendship, and are still dear friends and working partners. And we continue to talk nearly every day, about everything.

Part of this is having an interest in the world around us, and having a passion about things. It's hard to develop WordFood if you aren't engaged in something. In order to have a vocabulary you need an active existence, which goes back to what you let into your world. How expansive is it? How broad are the highways that reach into the rooms of your inner life? If you hide out at home in front of your computer all the time it's going to stunt your world, your horizons, your options, as well as your social competence. If emails and tweets are your only interactions with other people and surfing the Net is your only adventure, perhaps it's time to venture out.

Our creativity is sparked off one another. We are inspired by one another. We are amused by one another. Belly laughs are the product of the insanity of human beings. As convenient as it may be to work from home, we need the WordFood that we get every day from each other to survive and thrive. We need each other. And emails don't make up for it.

I hear people use email as an excuse to avoid taking responsibility.

> *"I sent him three emails. He hasn't replied. It's not my fault."*

> *"We sent you an email on this last week. You should have gotten it."*

And leaving voicemail messages is nearly as bad!

Then there is the issue about the email, voicemail or tweeting we'd like to have back. Back when we actually wrote letters, they took time for us to compose. When the bile came out, we reconsidered. We tore up the letter and started over. Not with today's instant communication. We say what we're thinking in that instant and wham! It's on its way to do real damage—not only to those who receive it but, in particular, to our reputation and the relationships we've built. Once it's gone, we can't reel it back in. We live to regret a foolish choice of words, a voicemail left in a fit of pique, an email fired off in anger. Technology and its speed are not always our friends.

In these cases we end up sending even more emails and voicemails in apology to make up for our blunders than if we had just picked up the damned phone and called someone.

How often is that anger based on misunderstanding an email because we didn't understand the emotion contained in it? We didn't hear the sarcasm or humor that the writer implied? Didn't get the joke? That's the bane of email—it can't convey emotions, and therefore a whole language has evolved to make up for what can't be conveyed otherwise (see below).

We need to hear WordFood from each other. We were born with a mouth and two ears for communication. It is beyond the pale that two people can sit in the same room texting one another. While that may be the fodder of late night comedians it is becoming a way of life for the up and coming generations who are fast losing the art of conversation. It is not only the ability to converse that they are losing, but the ability to read facial expressions and body language, those indicators of mood and changing emotions that are so critical to understanding our fellow human beings. With younger people spending most of their time staring at inanimate screens instead of human faces, there is no feedback. There is the potential of having an entire generation growing up without key knowledge of how to interact with one another. This has already shown up in the lack of basic customer service skills, so necessary to front line jobs in restaurant and hotel industries, just as an example. These young people are ill-equipped to handle the delicacies of human demands placed on them when customers have issues, and they feel put upon and angry when faced with emotional clients. They are much more comfortable in front of a computer, which doesn't talk back. Their range of WordFood is understandably limited when their language consists of acronyms.

P911, 4COL. B4N

"Parent in the Room, for Crying out Loud, Bye for Now."

In the military we had acronyms for everything. We talked about our CO (Commanding Officer) and going on TDY (temporary duty) and getting things done ASAP (as soon as possible). Some of those have been commonly adopted into everyday language. Every industry has its own language of acronyms. The demands of brevity for technology has caused kids to learn a whole new language.

This is a sampling of the 1,301 Text messaging entries found on the Web:

?4U	I have a question for you
<3	Meaning "sideways heart" (love, friendship)
</3	Meaning "broken heart"
14AA41	One for all, and all for one
1DR	I wonder
2G2BT	Too good to be true
A3	Anytime, anywhere, anyplace
AAK	Asleep at keyboard
AAMOF	As a matter of fact
ABC	Already been chewed
ADAD	Another day, another dollar
ADBB	All done, bye-bye
ADIH	Another day in hell
ADIP	Another day in paradise
AFZ	Acronym Free Zone
AFPOE	A fresh pair of eyes
AITR	Adult in the room
ATEOTD	At the end of the day
AYSOS	Are you stupid or something?
AYTMTB	And you're telling me this because
B9	Boss is watching
BASOR	Breathing a sigh of relief
BCNU	Be seeing you
BFFLNMW	Best friends for life, no matter what
BIC	Butt in chair
BOSMKL	Bending over smacking my knee laughing
BPLM	Big person little mind
BSOD	Blue screen of death
BYTM	Better you than me

You get the idea. If you're familiar with this code, then you're a seasoned texter, and this is no big deal to you. What has happened to your language skills since you've been using texts as a way to communicate regularly? Have you noticed anything that has changed? National Public Radio ran a story about people who had noticed differences in their cognitive abilities since spending a lot of time surfing the Internet. Their ability to focus and stay on a single topic had suffered significantly. When we don't write in a disciplined way, regularly, the skill gets rusty. When we don't speak with eloquence in a regular way, we lose the ability to communicate eloquently. *Pick up the damned phone and talk to someone.* Better still, make a date to meet for coffee and actually see them face to face.

There are several movies that have been made about brave young souls who have gone out to meet the people who have "friended" them on Facebook. This is being treated as a new concept: actually going out and meeting people face to face! Granted, Facebook is a construct of the twenty-first century, with all its opportunities and inherent dangers. What is being touted here is the grand adventure of a nerd going out to actually talk to people whom she only knows via the computer. This is only laughable because a while back this was called "life." It even had its own magazine.

Earlier in the book we talked about the WordFood we allow in through television and radio and movements we join. Email and tweets are daily bombardment by the hundreds. It is up to us to determine what part of that enormous avalanche of information is worth our attention. What of all that material actually feeds us? Who can you trust? Who is giving you something of value that will feed your heart and soul and not waste your time and money?

Language gives us the art to describe our inner lives, ourselves, our surroundings and our world. It gives us the ability to touch each other and lift each other up. Technology with its demands for brevity undermines the beauty of language. I'm not saying don't use technology or to not be competent in its ways. I'm saying don't lose the gift of eloquence, the beauty of good grammar, the competence of correct spelling and the erudite use of the well-turned phrase. This is great WordFood, too.

OH, *MOM!*

Life is made up of the moments that we spend being loved. More and more kids are committing suicide or becoming bullies or shooting each other because they are lonely and misunderstood. Where are they spending their time? In front of screens that don't hug back. And we are letting them. We give them more and more technology because it's cool, because they ask for it. Because all the newest and latest gadgets promise that we can stay in touch even better. However there is nothing that replaces human conversation, the WordFood that we feed each other based in love and respect. There is nothing that replaces the hugs that go with an "I love you," "Welcome home, honey" or "I missed you." It's not just the opportunity to remember those we are losing to old age and Alzheimer's, it's the hours and days and weeks of the growing up years that our kids are being shoved in front of the TV or given play toys to divert their attention while we…what? Do something more important than attend to our offspring? Watch them grow up? Set an example?

So how much time are our kids spending calling and texting? According to the Pew Research Center's Internet & American Life Project Surveys:

75% of teens 12-17 own cell phones, up from 45% in 2004. 88% are texters.

One in three teens between the ages of 12 and 17 sends more than 100 texts a day, or over 3,000 texts a month.

54% of teens use texts daily as of September 2009

38% of all teens call on the cell phone, and more girls than boys use the cell phone for calls.

Only 11% of teens use email.

Girls more fully embrace most aspects of cell-based communication. They send and receive about 80 texts a day compared to boys, who send 30.

In this era of texting and cell phones, parents regulate the cell phone use of their kids regularly. They stay in touch with their offspring, which is often the primary reason to have the cell phone in the first place. They also restrict their use, which has little effect on these statistics.

This is a lot of phone time for your teens and 'tweens, including in their cars, to our increasing concern.

52% of teens 16-17 have talked on a cell phone while driving.

48% of all teens have been in a car where the driver was texting.

40% of all teens say they have been in a car where the driver used the cell phone in a way that put themselves or others in danger.

The more gadgets, iphones, cell phones and distractions we give our kids, the more we have to compete for their face time. Find a way to get between your tween's gadget and her face to remind her that actual humans love and care about her. Communicate about the dangers of texting and driving.

She may complain, "Oh, *Mom!*" but it will matter, and she will remember.

CHAPTER NINE

WordFood Across Generations

It's in the positive daily WordFood that we create the sense of worth that kids need so much, and hold up the mirror to their value. Far more than adults, kids at all ages need to be told about their importance, and they cannot get this input from technology. Being connected to their friends may be terribly important to them, but approval from Mom, Dad, teachers and coaches, whoever the important people are in their lives, is paramount. They are constantly in need of WordFood to feed them something positive to live on.

Kids need and want feedback from their family about their intrinsic worth. This WordFood forms the backbone of how they feel about themselves. While there are some good WordFood sources out there in terms of television programming, there is simply nothing that replaces healthy family interchange. If family is toxic, then exchanges with positive adult figures, at school, church or counseling centers are key. Wherever children can get access to positive conversations, the kind of WordFood that gives them hope about themselves and their future, is a source of support.

If by any chance you have the time or inclination to make yourself available to a child through a program such as Big Brother, Big Sister, this is a huge gift. Your ability to bring WordFood to a child who desperately needs it could make all the difference. While you might have plenty to do in your life, and a great many demands on your time, there is little more important than to mentor a child.

WordFood changes lives, as we have already made clear, and this is an area where you can easily make a huge difference in a human life. And you have no idea where that child will go because of the difference you have made. As we have said, children learn their WordFood from us—so at every opportunity, let us give them shining examples.

It was a bit rough for me growing up. There was alcoholism in my family so I left home when I was barely sixteen. I was lucky to have a lot of kind people take an interest in my welfare along the way. They didn't want to change me or turn me in, they just wanted me to be safe and succeed in life. I always felt protected and safe through the early seventies because there were people like that in Ocala and St. Petersburg and Tampa and Orlando where I spent my late teens finishing high school on my own and working my way through the early days of college. I found ways to work and pay for a place to live but there were always families who made room for me in their homes.

Be the kind of person who makes room for kids at your house. Listen to that child's stories and by all means feed her WordFood about her worth. You can't know how important your kindness can be in the long run. Most of the people who helped me are now long gone, their kids all grown and moved away. I wish I had stayed in touch, for I owe them a great debt, and wish that I could let them know how grateful I am for their generosity.

While we owe our WordFood to everyone we meet, we especially owe it to our children, any child. Especially one who is lost and in trouble. There are those singular children, like my cousin's son who was a sociopath, who are beyond reaching, but they are rare. In most cases, kids want to be seen, noticed, appreciated, acknowledged, valued, validated, just like we all do. Children need positive and loving WordFood to make a stable and loving world, or to make a rocky world come right.

Most of us are working through our own issues as we become parents, and all too often we take our issues out on our kids. In so many cases we are working out our parents' relationships in our own marriages, with our children as witnesses. We stumble through this completely asleep and flail at the bystanders along the way, the precious little ones we brought into the world, without even realizing what we are doing. There is collateral damage, even in the best of families, most of it verbal. WordFood can heal it, heaping servings of HeartBreads and Energy Enhancers, the loving words that create trust and connections, the daily reminders of love that we all need. The honest expression of remorse for hurtful words or deeds goes a long way.

When I have done exercises during my WordFood seminars, participants learned that one toxic WordFood comment, even a minor one, left a powerful impression. One positive WordFood compliment wasn't enough to undo the damage. It would take two, three, even as many as *ten* servings of positive, loving WordFood to make up for the single negative impression. So, while kids are quick to forgive, remember that they need a great deal of loving WordFood. If we've been negative to them, we've got to make up for lost ground and rebuild what we've torn down. That of course is also true for adults, but it is especially the case for children, whose self-images are so dependent upon our opinion. We simply have to wake up, get out of our own issues and show up for our kids. Their need for kindness and emotional maturity is greater than our working out our personal dramas on their time. Children are not ornaments to our lives that we trot out when it's convenient. They demand our attention and hard work and absolute commitment.

Even at sixteen I knew that I wasn't mother material, and as soon as I could get a doctor to agree to the procedure, had my tubes tied. I was 27. I was neither brave enough, nor strong enough, to bear the emotional and psychological weight of raising children. Luckily, I realized it early on and didn't make a family pay for my incompetence in this essential arena. I leave it to mothers to do the mothering, but I decry those who shirk their responsibility once they have had children. We owe them our best every single day. I know what it looks like. I've met some good ones over the years.

One adopted mother of mine is Marge Hempstead (not her real name), who is in her mid-eighties. If you met her you would think she was in her sixties. She is slim, athletic, vivid, intense and brilliant. She works out daily, does yoga, runs, lifts weights and operates several international businesses. She grew up with a family that honored brains in women, a family that regularly fed her powerful WordFood. She is a perfect example of what happens when a child's self-image is supported fully and she was reinforced from a young age. As a child, she knew Franklin Roosevelt and was a guest at the White House. Marge is a financial and business mastermind and she is a great supporter of women. She has positively affected the lives of thousands of women in Colorado.

Years ago I was introduced to her when I was getting ready to go on an extended backpacking trip in Australia and New Zealand. I needed her advice on what to pack for every contingency. Being an outdoors person, she was an expert in such things. Thus began a thirty-year relationship that continues today.

Marge has advised me in business, been my mentor, my friend, my stand-in mother through the years, as I have lived through the death of my parents, the comings and goings of various boyfriends and the great Australia trip that lasted four years. Today she continues to advise, counsel, feed me WordFood that has helped me navigate an uncommon life. Despite the fact that I have always been her "nutty" friend Julia, she has never wavered in her support. Her love and approval mean the world to me. In Marge, I find the mother I've always wanted.

Can you be someone's Marge Hempstead? Can you be the steady, loving voice in someone's life? No matter how old a person is, we all need mentors. Now, in my late fifties, I still treasure a mother figure, even as I provide that for others. What WordFood are you willing to provide that will guide another's life? You have valuable wisdom that will help someone along the way, and the time you take to help, no matter how brief it may be, will be so appreciated.

Mentoring can happen at any time, in any environment. It doesn't have to be a lifetime commitment. It can be a one-time conversation. I've found myself in numerous situations where I've had a heartfelt conversation with someone in passing. Someone has either pulled me aside or we've found ourselves going deep into a discussion about something very personal. This has happened many times in my travels. It's a chance to be very authentic with other human beings and I never shy away from it. In those moments I open my heart completely. It's unlikely I will see or hear from them again, but sometimes I do. What I know is that those exchanges can make all the difference in a person's life. When we're willing to be emotionally open, to be totally honest with people and let them be themselves with us, it is a jewel box moment. It can be transforming instead of transactional. Who's to say a person isn't contemplating suicide and that person's conversation with us is what is going to keep him or her from acting on that thought? Who's to say that person's talk with us is what is going to help make an important decision about an unborn child? Mentoring happens over bottled water, a chance latte in a coffee shop, or around the office copier. People everywhere are hungry for positive WordFood all the time. Your willingness to be genuine can alter the course of a life. Never underestimate the power of your ability to affect someone. This is why your ability with language is so important; there are people in pain all around us, people who need you and your thoughtful WordFood.

At a recent conference, I mentioned to a group of students that I had backpacked around Australia alone for four years. Later, one of the young women approached me. She said she was about to head for the north of Spain on a long trek, and needed some advice on what to pack for her journey. Happy to be of assistance, I sat down with her and we went over the list of key components she needed. We also discussed how to travel safely and ways to enjoy her journey. We made instant friends, and agreed that she would stay in touch. I told her the story about my friend Marge. History was repeating itself.

Later that evening I called Marge. "You'll never guess what happened today," I said. "I sure thought of you!" I told her the story of the student's backpacking trip and we laughed. We are sure that this young woman will become a mentee of mine, as I am of Marge's. Another relationship, beginning with a little advice for an overseas journey, with the potential of lasting a lifetime.

There is a young woman in my family who has recently come upon some books and ideas that are changing her life. I possess a considerable amount of training in this particular area and we found ourselves discussing this on a recent visit. I hadn't been aware of her discoveries, and this newfound interest of hers delighted me. It is an area where I can be of real help and service, and it allows me to be closer to her and her young family in the process. Through providing reading suggestions, a place to discuss ideas and challenge old ways of thinking, I can be a mentor to this lovely young woman. This will push me as well, to be judicious and careful not to let my ego get in the way of being a good teacher. Whether within your own family, at school, at your child's school or in a library, a park bench or bumping into someone in a cafeteria, you never know where your chance to be a mentor might come. Take it. To be of service to another human being is what we came here to do. It will feed you like no other activity you do in life.

Food for Thought

When you offer your advice or ideas to other people, keep in mind that a part of them is always going to hear what you are offering. It's taking it all in whether you're being thanked for your help or not. We all have personalities, and underneath these personas we have the subconscious, which recalls every single thing. Under deep hypnosis, we can recall the doctor's words as they brought us out of the womb. When you work with people, you may feel at times that your hard work is being ignored. This may be true of their personality. Their ego may be rejecting or questioning what you say. They may not be ready for what you're offering them. Perhaps they ignore your good advice. But be assured that what you say is landing on fertile ground at a deeper level. People act on information when they are ready and only then. You never know when they will have heard you—it may be months or years. But what you are saying is landing. Your challenge is to give up needing to take credit for helping them.

I have a friend who harbors great anger toward her brother, and we talk about forgiving him. She still refuses, but I know that at some level what I say matters. It's making sense. Not at the surface where her ego is engaged, but deeper, where her soul operates. She may or may not act on this. All I want her to do is hear the words. Then I let it go.

Older people sometimes have a hard time taking advice or counsel from younger people, especially their kids, whom they have counseled all their lives. To accept their kids' advice is to admit to being old, or to not have all the wisdom. So they may not openly acknowledge when their child is right. That doesn't mean they didn't hear or inwardly value what their child said or did.

You don't have to shout, argue or pontificate to make your point. You will be heard. What's important is to let go of the need to be acknowledged for making a difference in a person's life. That's your ego talking, and, again, being a mentor is not about your ego, it's about service to another.

CHAPTER TEN

Wrapping It Up

If you've read through this book and are now thinking about all the people in your life who could benefit from some healthy WordFood and you are going to go change them, wait a minute. First and foremost, feed yourself healthy WordFood. It all starts with you.

What we've been saying throughout this book is feed yourself first from the wonderful healthy foods of the WordFood Pyramid so that you can start the day feeling loved and regarded. Then, depending on your belief system, add to this some words that uplift and guide you and provide you with the sense that you are protected and safe.

Next you take this out into the day, where you are now better able to handle the WordFood Diets you encounter. You also are now better able to meet the challenges of the people who deserve your compassion and understanding and the best Balanced WordFood Diet you can feed them.

As you speak healthy WordFood every day, it will strengthen you mentally, emotionally and spiritually. You will gain from every word you utter, offered from clear and pure intentions. Every time you stand in the face of anger and protect another's dignity, you will grow and that person will be grateful. Every time you coach a young person and he or she takes a better path you will grow and both will be grateful. WordFood will feed you first and foremost, and you will come to love yourself and trust your heart. It will come easily to you. Let's look at some of the other take-home lessons.

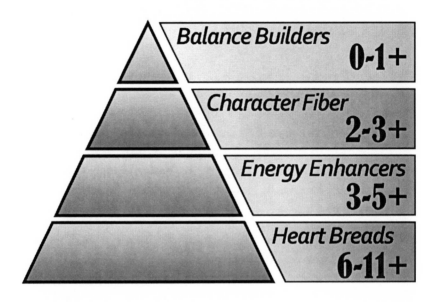

Let others receive your WordFood without expectations that they must change or respond

An important lesson of WordFood is to offer it to others with the understanding that they may not accept it, understand it or appreciate it. They may respond in disgust and hate. There is no guarantee that your precious gift will be well received and "digested" as intended. As every great teacher has learned in his or her own way, people hear what they are ready to hear and no more. It is not about you, it is about the willingness to serve. You have done what you can and what is right, and that is all you can do—for yourself, your family, your friends, your peers, your work group, your community. It's not about being right, it's about being your best in every way you can be.

It's also not your role to be an evangelist, to force people to draw from the Balanced WordFood Diet. It's your role to hold your own space, to love and express love, to communicate from a place of clarity and compassion. To keep people whole when you speak to them, and to ensure that they feel good when they leave your presence. That you listen to understand, that others feel heard and valued. That is enough in and of itself, an invitation to another life, another way of being in the world. People will more likely be drawn by a quiet power and love than by any convincing on your part. Remember, that is behavior closely related to the Devil's Food WordFood Diet, and you don't need to go there.

Be prepared to leave old relationships behind

As you begin to draw from the WordFood Pyramid every day, you will find your eloquence and your relationships begin to shift. There may even be some significant changes in your life and your connections. People are likely to respond to you differently, more warmly, with more openness and regard. You may find yourself surrounded by different kinds of people. Don't be surprised if you are drawn to a new kind of people in your life as you find old styles of relating unacceptable. It will be like shedding an old skin and entering a new life.

As this happens, you may find that some friends and acquaintances may pressure you. They will not want you to change, so they try to keep you in your old habits, your old ways of being. This won't serve you anymore. While this may be difficult, it's best to let those friendships go and welcome healthier, more productive friendships into your life. Find people who want to communicate at this newer, different WordFood level. You will feed each other the food of mutual regard. As a result, you will live a different kind of life that results in greater happiness, satisfaction and contentment. This may bring up some sadness for you for the relationships you are leaving behind, which is normal and understandable. But think also about what you are gaining, and the quality of life you are moving toward.

This book has invited you not only to speak differently but also to engage yourself at different levels. It has asked you to consider seeing some of your communications with others as opportunities to experience your courage, your gentility, your kindness even in the face of another's bad behavior. When you do these things you grow in amazing ways.

Let your words be of service

The WordFood Pyramid is the language of service. The more you speak it, the more you will find yourself wanting to find ways to make a difference, wanting to give rather than get. The highest kind of existence in this life is that of service to our fellow man. It is through the many servings of warmth, graciousness, love and caring you offer that you see the call to service and find your way to make a difference. My beloved coach Lari Mangum says, "Every interaction is an opportunity to help the human condition." With that in mind, you can consider every single conversation you have an opportunity to leave someone elevated. What an extraordinary thought. Done without selfish motivation, your acts of kindness can grace everyone you meet, and have transformative value.

If you recall, we said earlier that you cannot give this kind of gift without having it affect you. So each gift of kindness touches you as well, and transforms you in the giving. Every time you add value to another's life, you add value to your own.

Part of this is finding ways to put business aside at the office and taking the time to just listen to someone's issue, or offer a hug (if policy allows). Sit down with others and hear about their lives. The work will get done. For everyone who is working, there is an average backlog of nineteen hours of unfinished tasks. That means none of us will ever be fully caught up. Why not take the time right now to do the most important thing, which is to be here for each other? Make space for your humanity and let people be themselves around you. Business is nothing more than people being with people. You will find that, when you make this investment, productivity will go up. When you do this at home, you will find your family acting more like family instead of a group of loosely related human beings who look alike.

Set an example for the kids

We set the example for how our kids learn to treat others. And how we treat our children is perhaps the greatest teacher of all. How we speak to them teaches them the art of words, tone and body language. We have all laughed as our tiny children mimic our phrases and tones, and we have rolled our eyes or been horrified as they have also copied some of our worst behavior. They miss nothing, and emulate everything.

What are you feeding *your* children? Are you cascading down what you learned from your parents? Or will you break that pattern?

Children learn tolerance when they are fed tolerance. They learn love when they are fed love. They learn patience when they experience patience. They learn hate when they experience it themselves. They learn to despise themselves when they are met with disapproval from their parents.

It all begins with your relationship with yourself in the mirror, every single day. It isn't magic. It is the everyday choice you make to love yourself. To treat yourself with regard and respect. When you take on this responsibility seriously and live your life out of love, then you will treat your loved ones the same way. Your children will learn to love themselves by watching how you love yourself. It takes courage to face yourself every single day with acceptance. Your "Master Architect" does, and so should you. Your children look to you for the best example, and this is your highest gift to them.

It is a fact of life that when our teenagers hit puberty, they will begin to rebel. The natural process of evolution forces them to move away from us and leave home to become adults on their own. The disagreements that are part of being teenagers are part of the essential disintegration of the close family unit. Kids have to leave to make their own way. And parents must trust that they have trained their children well enough to succeed. If the children were fed good WordFood, shown good WordFood examples along the way, they will have good self-esteem. They will know how to treat others well. And they'll re-enter their parents' lives with success stories soon enough.

CHAPTER ELEVEN

Authentic Conversations

How did I come to write a book about words? Over the years my life has been enriched by many, many stories and examples from others whose lives were enhanced by—and sometimes brought down by—their words. These stories have much value for us all. Here are a few of those stories.

WHY LATER IS TOO LATE

Recently, a friend wrote to tell me that her stepson, an otherwise apparently healthy young man in his thirties, had suddenly died, leaving a three-year-old son and a young wife.

I thought about that young man and wondered if anyone had recently fed him the kind of WordFood that made his heart sing. Had anyone said, "I love you, I treasure you"? What were the last things he heard before he died? Was he thinking about the list of things he had to get done, work projects, an empty gas tank? No one can possibly know. But if he had time to think, he was probably thinking of those he loved, and what he most wanted to say to them. Just as those he loved are now thinking about all the things they wish they had said to him now that he is gone.

With hours, minutes, seconds to live, I doubt we will waste time thinking about the Haynes project or the busted door jamb. We will think about the loved ones in our lives and what we need to say to them, the longing in our hearts, the secrets we need to express. When it comes down to the bare essentials, it comes down to love.

Why do we wait until the last moment? Or, worse, until it's too late?

Last year another friend lost a brother of 41 to a heart attack. Michael was heartbroken not only for the good times lost, but for all the important things left unsaid. All the important words of respect, acknowledgment and regard between brothers. They had not spoken for several years and Michael now feels the weight of those years like lead in his heart.

In our culture we assume today that we're going to live until we are at least in our eighties or nineties. With the miracles of science and good nutrition and exercise, we are lulled into thinking we are invincible. But we are not. Every day people we love develop diseases, drop dead, have strokes, move away, fade away. We lose important opportunities to say what we need to say to people. We have arguments, our pride gets in the way, we get busy, we forget. We *forget*. And then suddenly, they are gone forever, and what we have left are regrets for all the chances we had to have meaningful conversations. These moments are now lost to us, to say the things that truly meant something. Heal a wound, mend a hurt, express a love, forgive a misunderstanding—WordFood can do it all—before someone leaves our lives. And if they don't leave, all the better. They remain and we are communicating with them in a much healthier way. The point is to treat each other with the recognition that each moment with them is priceless, because it is priceless. The ever-present, ever-changing *now*, never to be had again, is a jewel in time. *Now* is always available to take Word-Food and transform a relationship through an authentic conversation and take it to a wholly different level.

"Later" is too late. We don't have time to "get around to it." Before you know it twenty years have passed and your brother is dying of cancer halfway across the country. Your beloved grade school teacher you always meant to call passed away four years ago. The guy you served with overseas moved one more time, and this time he didn't send you the forwarding address because you failed to write. People fall away from us like autumn leaves to be swept up by the haunting wind of regret. What you have is right now, and now is the time to say the WordFood that has to be said.

My friend Jeff told me about the difficulties he had with his long-time roommate Allen. For the past year, Jeff had increasingly grown tired of his friend's habits—even to the point that Jeff would some-times find excuses to stay elsewhere rather than be around Allen. He felt that Allen was completely to blame for the falling out, yet Jeff never said anything to him. He just let his own bad feelings fester.

When Jeff heard that Allen had taken a new job out of the country and was leaving for good, still Jeff said nothing. Rather than explaining why he had been so distant lately, Jeff passed on this opportunity to clear the air. Allen left and will probably never know the real reason for the cold shoulders and bitter, sarcastic sniping Jeff had showered on him. Today Jeff wonders if he should have said *something*.

My friend Debbie's mother, Edith, is 84 and fading into dementia. Debbie's father died when she was 29, so she and her mother have been inseparable ever since. They have always lived close to each other, eaten together, shopped, talked and lived their lives nearly as sisters. Now Edith is wearing diapers and Debbie is faced with her mother's imminent death.

Debbie was getting furious with her mother's frequent accidents and for her mother's stuffing her diapers into the cat's kitty litter box. There were other offenses, usually a result of her mother's increasing inability to take care of herself. This led to arguments and accusations and great unhappiness on both sides. One day Debbie and I sat down and explored the fact that her mother was not going to get better. This was one problem that she would not be able to fix with her considerable intellect—and no amount of guile and problem solving on her part would reverse her mother's deteriorating condition.

This loving perspective changed everything. Debbie was able to visit her mother and forgive her for getting older—and ultimately, for leaving her alone. That was the *real* issue. Debbie was afraid of being left by herself, which is her great adult journey. This isn't her mother's fault. For now, while her mother is still alive, she is treating her with loving WordFood and kindness. This means patience and understanding, and much good humor. There are more good days than bad. She realizes that Edith is going to ultimately leave her behind but anger would have cost her precious time while her mother is still able to interact. And happily, she is wise enough to take advantage of those important moments. WordFood is healing them for what is going to be a great step for them both.

A cousin of mine told me the story about her beloved second husband, Danny. Ellen and Danny had a volatile relationship, full of arguments and fights. The source of the fights was Danny's son, a sociopath and pathological liar, who caused them continual heartache. Danny was under considerable stress on the job, and his only outlet was Ellen. For ten years, despite the love they felt for each other, their relationship was defined by huge, hurtful battles, toxic WordFood that left them exhausted. At one point, Ellen was left so damaged by Danny's verbal outbursts that she found herself curled up in a fetal position, unable to go on. Unwilling to end the marriage but convinced that the way they were going was untenable, she demanded, and got, a separation.

During the separation, two things happened. Danny showered her with cards, flowers and pleas for reconciliation. This was too much Ice Cream & Cake; too much, too late. The marriage counselor advised him to stop, and give Ellen some time and space. In the meantime, Ellen met someone new and had an affair.

The combination of the time away and the affair made Ellen realize how much she loved Danny and wanted him back. They reconciled.

One month later Danny was diagnosed with terminal cancer. It was devastating to the newly reunited couple. Suddenly Danny and Ellen found the WordFood to communicate with love, patience and understanding despite the challenging son. They were able to navigate the difficult corridors of their relationship with open hearts. In the final months of their time together, they shared the kind of connection that had always been possible but somehow just out of reach during the previous nearly twelve years.

Why does it take imminent loss to force us to find the language of love that is in our hearts, desperate to be expressed? For ten years, Danny and Ellen fought instead of cherishing each other. It took separation, and then cancer, for them to find the Word-Food of respect and regard. How many couples are living with locked horns instead of locked lips? It is criminal that we waste years in battle with those we love when those precious weeks, months and years could have been spent sharing hugs, laughter, sweet glances of understanding.

Is your life built around blaming someone else for what is not right in your life? Are you, like Danny and Ellen, locked in a war where love is trapped between the lines of battle that only disaster can free? Are you, like Jeff, invested in a "story" in which the other was the wrong-doer? Earlier in the book we discussed this as "singing your song." Do you spend precious lifetime singing your song about how others have done you wrong and you are the central character in a drama? Here is where WordFood can free you, give you your life back, if you have the courage to see things as they are instead of as you would have them be in your story.

This step will take considerable courage on your part, especially if you have built an entire life, a whole persona, around your story. If your picture of yourself is based on being a victim, real or imaginary, letting go of this essential theme in your life is going to leave you adrift for a while until you build a new foundation of your own. You will need to write a new story line for yourself. Who are you without a perpetrator that you can blame for the lack in your life, all your ills and losses? What happens if you begin to see that you were perpetrating this on yourself, that no one was doing this to yourself but you, and you were the victimizer all along? This is where you realize that you are using toxic WordFood to keep yourself from being all you can be, and blaming others for what is wrong in your own life. What freedom to catch yourself in the act, and to finally stop. What a brave new world to step into as master of your own life, able to feed yourself WordFood of encouragement and care.

Sometimes a good friend, loved one or family member won't allow us the chance to make things right. My big brother chooses to be a stranger to me, and I have no way to reach him. There is much WordFood that needs to be said between us that would heal this relationship, but he chooses to keep the door closed. In cases like this, all you can do is speak the WordFood to the loved one in your heart, and offer up the caring and emotion that you would otherwise express in person. Say what needs to be said as though your loved one was right there. If necessary, get someone close to you to act out the part of this loved one so that you have a person to speak the WordFood to. The important thing is to get out the words for your own sake. If you have absolutely no way to reach the other person, as I have with my big brother, all you can do is send out the love in your heart and soul. You need to forgive yourself for whatever you may have harbored against this person. Free yourself from the anger, guilt, remorse, bitterness, whatever emotions you've been carrying. You're the one bearing this burden, so let it go. When and if you see this person again you can welcome them with open arms and a free heart.

CAPTURE THE WORDFOOD WHILE YOU CAN

My coach Orvel Ray has an elderly neighbor who also has developed dementia. For twenty years they visited and told wonderful stories. Suddenly, his neighbor no longer recognizes him at all—while he is friendly and enthusiastic about visitors, gone are the terrific tales and the wonderful evenings filled with stories. And Orvel Ray wishes many times over that he had taken a recording device to get a record of this man's life events.

How many wonderful yarns of a life that has fast disappeared are gone forever because of this devastating disease? How many amazing storytellers have been silenced forever by this thief of tales? For many of us, the only history of our family that we will ever know exists in the memories of our grandparents, our uncles, aunts and cousins. We put them away in old folks' homes and let them decay there, along with all the precious information about where we come from, who we really are, the people who made up our history and gave us our faces, our bone structure, our personalities. The mysteries of our families and the keys to our character lie buried in the stories our kin can tell us, yet we are so quick to set them aside when they become burdensome and querulous and demanding. They alone can fill in the blanks, and we must hear them before they too go blank. They need our caring WordFood, the respect they deserve for the parts they have played in our lives. Tape their stories. Get them before they are gone. You may need to swallow your pride to do so, but you will always be glad you did.

WORDFOOD AND YOUR STORY

WordFood has the ability to completely change a mood and soothe a situation, as my friend Bill discovered recently.

Bill plays in a jazz band, where there are two other players who have distinctly different personalities. Buddy is positive, lighthearted and easygoing about their gigs, and he looks to get the best experiences out of all of them. Ed is the singer/songwriter, and he is the cynic, always finding something to gripe about: the lighting, the acoustics, the crowd.

The other day Bill was puzzling about why he got along fine with Buddy but not so well with Ed. Meanwhile, Ed complained about how Bill responded more positively to Buddy. The band has been together for several years and the relationships are strong and intimate. Bill said that the band had recently been asked to play an outdoor farmer's market. Unfortunately the organizer had failed to supply several of the key elements for the band, ranging from shade for them and their instruments, plywood to protect their expensive equipment from the dirt, or a stable platform for the drums. It hadn't even occurred to this guy to provide power for the amplifiers. The gig was unpaid. Still, Buddy enthusiastically went from one problem to the next, working out solutions, keeping Bill on track through his frustration. Meanwhile Ed constantly complained and talked about giving up and going home. Buddy's can-do attitude helped Bill focus on doing a professional job—which ultimately landed them a lead to a big opportunity at a large blues micro brewery. Bill recognized that it was Buddy's attitude and use of positive WordFood that had kept him focused on putting the show together, while Ed's cynical WordFood only compounded an already difficult situation. No wonder that Bill is naturally drawn to Buddy's collaborative, positive WordFood, which made the show possible (if not very comfortable) despite the poor conditions, and the entire day at the farmer's market worthwhile.

WordFood—how we posit things in our minds, how we frame situations in our inner worlds, the way Buddy was able to do at the farmer's market—is key. Instead of being defeated by an unpleasant situation he took one awkward moment after another and handled it with humor and aplomb. With his positive WordFood he was able to cajole Bill into a better state of mind. The band played well and a talent scout was very impressed. This would not have happened if Ed's negative WordFood and cynical attitude had won the day. No wonder Bill is drawn to Buddy rather than Ed.

How do you speak to yourself, frame things in your inner mind? Do you place yourself as the victim in life's situations on a regular basis or do you take responsibility for your role in life every day? Your inner WordFood makes all the difference.

Many times we are also telling others stories that we have been repeating for many years and it's time to change them. A good friend of mine, a trainer, was telling me that he recently received a missive from someone that contained a story this professional speaker had been telling for many years. While the story had a point, it was very outdated. This is like that old speaker's favorite, the story about the starfish on the beach that gets thrown back in the water by the little girl or boy because "it makes a difference to that one." This was a similar story, and was the man's signature story from forty years back.

What struck my friend was that at some point we simply have to change what we are telling people. We have to grow: become something new and evolve. It is imperative that we grow because that is life's imperative. As consultants to business, within our families, as providers of ideas or as friends to one another, we are always growing and changing. Life isn't static and neither are we. Our ideas—and our words—change as we constantly experience new things every day.

Are you telling the same story year after year? In your business? In your life?

It is very easy to get addicted to a theme that fits us. We find a story that echoes some aspect of our life and we snap it up as our own, and we continue to tell it to others because it gets a laugh or gets a response that we enjoy.

Last September, while helping a neighbor with his roof, a friend of mine fell some sixteen feet to the ground. At first, he thought he'd only sprained his ankle. Instead, he had not only broken his foot in several places, but also his arm and his back. Of course, everyone asked him "What happened?" and he would tell the story about how he managed to slip and fall, capping it with the punch line: "No good deed ever goes unpunished." This of course garnered a laugh.

The story doesn't end there. This man and his wife are activists and spend a great deal of time doing good deeds in many aspects of their lives. After several months of putting up with her husband's joke, she finally put her foot down. She pointed out that he wasn't supporting his healing with his words, and was basically inviting the Universe at large to strike him down again for all the good deeds they were doing in their lives. Realizing the wisdom of her insight, he stopped making the joke.

What kinds of stories do you tell about yourself that get laughs or responses that you enjoy? Do they support you? Really? Do they sustain who you are becoming, where you are headed in life? Listen to the words you are saying. Do they maintain a picture of you as a victim? I'm not talking about bragging. What I'm talking about is drawing a positive picture of yourself in life that is worth developing. What is the life story that you tell others? What kind of reaction do you ask for and get? What do you elicit from others when you use WordFood with them? What is your intention?

During the process of the writing of this book I hit a point where I was stuck. I found myself repeating the words "I hit a wall, I hit a wall." The more I repeated the toxic WordFood, the more the words made it true, and the more stuck I became. How many times have you told yourself a story that you brought into being and it became true for you? It wasn't until my coach pointed out what I was doing to myself—feeding myself negative WordFood—that I stopped, and of course the negative process stopped as well. What stories are you feeding yourself that are keeping you from moving forward in your life?

People get deeply invested in the stories they tell about themselves, and sometimes the stories become more important than the person. That's when it's time to let the story go and start living again. We all know the faded high school quarterback who relives his glory days at the corner bar, or the beauty queen who came in second in her twenties and now in her forties is still bitter about it. What kind of WordFood are these people feeding themselves that it is spilling out as moldy recyclables? When you look in the mirror do you still see an 18-year-old football player when everyone else sees a 38-year-old accountant? Even though it might be hard to hear, what are you telling yourself, honestly, that needs to be updated?

This conversation with ourselves is critical if we are going to be authentic with others. We must be truthful with ourselves, the one person we cannot escape. We must be honest about who we are and how we show up in the world. This includes our character, our foibles and our idiosyncrasies. How we probably aren't Superman or Superwoman after all, despite our fondest childhood dreams. Learning to be brutally honest with ourselves takes a lifetime, but the best time to start is now.

We start with understanding that we are not going to be perfect, live forever, win the Olympic gold (unless you actually have), get and maintain a model's body until you're 95, or any of the other lies that ads have told us. That's toxic WordFood, untruths that

Madison Avenue has fed us that get us to buy products. We are, and can always be, pretty amazing, capable, good people who go out and make a difference every day in each other's lives. Without, by the way, being perfect, living forever, winning the gold, having a model's body or anything else that the products promise.

The time that we spend aching for something other than what we are or have could be spent learning to love ourselves, feeding ourselves loving WordFood, which would make ourselves easier to live with. Loving WordFood makes our living environment happy for however long we are alive. It's not about being perfect; it's about being perfectly happy with what we are given every day. That's perspective, and that's all about WordFood, how we teach ourselves to see. The daily conversation that we have with ourselves determines our quality of life. It is the internal environment of the soul, where we hold forth conversations with our Master Architect or hold our most precious beliefs. How holy is this place inside you? What kind of altar do you place your thoughts upon? Is your inner world a cauldron of anger and blame? Or have you come to a sense of peace and balance?

Another question is the breadth of our vocabulary. Hear how you describe yourself and your circumstances to others. Do you use the same adjectives, the same adverbs, the same exact story over and over again? Has it gotten tattered with the telling? One cure for this is to expand your vocabulary as you retell your story. And to retell your story with different outcomes.

I'M *NOT* SHY

As I was writing this book, I was going back over certain aspects of my early life. I had always told people I'd been very shy. But when I looked back at the facts of my teens—moving out and making friends and living on my own and adopting families—those aren't the actions of a painfully shy kid. I had to face my "story" and reconsider this version of my life. It simply wasn't true, and discovering that was liberating. What part of your story do you tell in order to get what you want, but it isn't true? What part of your story doesn't feed you, help you move forward? What's keeping you in jail? Are you so caught up in your story that you don't quite even remember the truth yourself? I was. And it took writing this book for me to remember the facts of my own life and be freed by them.

THIS INNER PLACE

This inner place is the one you face when you look at yourself in the mirror every morning. Interestingly, it is also the one we come face to face with every time we have a conversation with someone. Every time we talk to someone, that person holds up a mirror. What we say in anger to someone else, we are in truth saying to ourselves. What we accuse others of goes for ourselves as well. Those who participate with us in conversation are observers to our conversations with self. They are our guides, our mentors, our mirrors, whether we realize it or not. And they are to be respected as such.

So often when we speak, we think our WordFood is intended for the listener when in truth, it is for us to hear. We speak for ourselves. We need to hear our words, speak our truths, hear ourselves think out loud, while others validate us with their presence. If we possess wisdom, even in anger we know that what we say is self-directed, and that our conversational partner can only bear witness to our frustration with ourselves. When we are being authentic, when we are not spinning a story, we know this to be true. That's why in most every case, when we are angry it's about us, and our feelings, not about someone else. That truth will set you free from your stories, the toxic WordFood that you feed yourself that can keep you from moving forward in life.

WATCH OUT FOR YOUR PARTS

Remember earlier in the book when we talked about your different parts, the different aspects of yourself that have different voices that sometimes act in opposition to you? This is a good place to revisit that notion. These different factions—all very much you but sometimes not always acting in your best interest—can pipe up sometimes and be telling stories to get attention because it's fun and entertaining and makes friends for you but it also draws an unhealthy picture of you. Be watchful of who's talking at any given time, especially after a social drink or two or three. Remember, many communities live inside you and they don't always speak as one. Some of them aren't very wise. Some of them are very manipulative with other's emotions. Those are the storytellers, and they can be great liars. Those are the ones you want to keep in check.

HOW VARIED IS YOUR EXPRESSIVE RANGE?

"I love you" is important, but hundreds of ways exist to express your affection beyond those three words and a bouquet of red roses. Books of poetry and verse, for example. Shakespeare wrote great sonnets, the Bible is full of gorgeous songs; you can find innumerable ways to state how you feel. Don't limit yourself. The broader the variety the more fun it is to say. Look for new ways to authentically express yourself and to keep your love language fresh and exciting. Say something specific about the things you appreciate that your beloved does. This keeps it very personal and special between you. Make it your purpose to find a new way to say you care by reading how the great writers write. It will give you pleasure and some wonderful ideas of your own.

EGO AND PRIDE

It is true that some people will go to their death before they will accept an apology, end a fight or offend their pride. This is the ego's great triumph over life's potential on this earth, its greatest victory over happiness and love. Countless people have chosen to suffer because they could not utter the WordFood of forgiveness to their children, their family members, their spouses. They chose ego over elation, and the world was poorer for it. Don't be fooled by your ego into losing precious time isolating yourself from others. If you find yourself behaving like some of the diets described in this book, and most everyone does, it's time to ask what you are losing as a result. What does your pride or anger cost you? What is the price of fear or hatred? Who truly is hurt when we withhold words of forgiveness and caring? It's not only the other person—we suffer, too. In fact, in most cases, we suffer far more than the person we are trying to hurt, as in my cousin Jeff's case with his roommate.

My father was an alcoholic, and when I was in my forties I called him on it. It had turned him into something unpleasant and mean, and I finally screwed up the courage to say something to him. I asked him to please treat me like an adult, to which he said, "I can't do that." The result of the conversation was disastrous. My father ultimately banned me from the family, refused to let my mother talk to me for a very long time and then for years we had no contact at all until he was riddled with cancer and near death. His last act of violence was to write me out of his will. I was allowed to see him one more time before he died, and it was a sad and controlled exchange. Shortly afterward he was gone. So were all his stories of being a roommate with Hollywood legends Jimmy Stewart, Burgess Meredith and Henry Fonda in the 1920s, being the first TV announcer for the Redskins in 1948, when newsman David Brinkley was still a copy boy. He had led an amazing life and I had learned very little of it, because of his pride.

Over the years I did try to have adult conversations with my father on many occasions. I would sit down with him when I would come home from the Army on leave while my parents were at a vacation destination or at home in Florida. My father would have his drink in hand, and I would strike up a discussion about work or football. He would regale me with tales of their five-wheeler travels, as my father was fond of being the center of attention, the storyteller. Then I would try to steer the conversation to something more substantial, like feelings about my relationship with him, and how we got along. More specifically, his role in our relationship, and his abusive behavior of me once I had become an adult. Instantly he would clam up and walk out of the room. Often he would go into the bathroom and turn on the tub as though to take a bath. My father didn't take baths.

This man's wall was impenetrable. It became evident that alcohol was a factor. I tried talking with him before evening drinks, and that was even worse. My father still got up and walked out of the room, a rude gesture to anyone, family or not. I was pursuing my need to get closer to my father, to have some sort of communion with him, which might lead to a father-daughter connection. I wanted a relationship that went beyond his verbal abuse of me in front of my husband and friends. I was interested in his stories and background, but not at the expense of my getting publicly shamed. That was when, in a clumsy attempt to make progress, I pointed out that he was an alcoholic, which injured his pride far worse than anything else I might have said. That's what ultimately led to my estrangement from the family.

My father was punishing me for the things I had said to him. But his form of punishment cost us both a relationship for the rest of his life. Instead of finding a way to talk about it, my dad shut the door and I lost my family for years. He was unwilling to talk to me, to hear me out. Part of this was his generation but most of it was his pride. He never found out about the woman I was becoming, and I think he would have been proud. I'd have liked that a lot.

When someone else is too committed to being right, too invested in their point of view, you're not going to get heard. I probably didn't possess the best WordFood skills at that point in life but I did care, and I had the desire to connect with my father. Desire just wasn't enough. Sometimes it takes a mediator just to start the conversation. Every situation is unique. And everyone in your life needs something different from you. Some want your approval, some want your love, some just want money. You need to be smart enough to know the difference.

MONEY AND WORDFOOD

Money was used in my family in lieu of love. Dad dangled dollars in front of the kids as a way of keeping us close. There were many gifts at Christmas, an embarrassment of riches. My mother told me much later that it was an apology for the previous year. It would have been better to have had a nice year and a slimmer Yule. My parents lent money to us and kept careful records, and we were reminded of the debts. Mine were paid off and my father showed a combination of grudging respect and displeasure, displeasure because this could no longer be held over my head.

Be careful that you aren't being manipulated for money in your relationships, whether in the family or through friends, where love is being professed. It's an ugly trick. Toxic WordFood and well-crafted phrases make you feel guilty.

My girlfriend has a brother who worked his aged mother for all the investments left to her for her life care by convincing her time and again that he needed them for a broken down car, or rent, or some emergency. Over time he bilked her out of everything this widow had left until another family member took the checkbook out of her hands and all her financials out of reach. She was left to live on Social Security and very little else. This man was perfectly capable of taking care of himself, he was able-bodied and working. He just didn't want to. He had a free ride, and took advantage of it. To his mother, the disingenuous WordFood sounded convincing, and it worked.

To so many who are vulnerable, to lonely family members, the aged, the needy and especially to those family members who feel a measure of guilt for some past misdeed, toxic WordFood can work to wean out of them the last life savings. In some cases they need to be protected from themselves by other family members, lawyers or good friends who step in and take charge. If you have someone like this in your life, ask the hard questions about what is going on. Uncover whether that person is being drained of their resources by someone who is using false love as a way of getting money. Protect them from themselves. It may take a tough WordFood conversation, it may be painful, but it has to be done. These bloodsuckers won't stop until the last penny has been taken from their marks. This is one of the worst uses of toxic WordFood, when people prey on the weak, especially members of their own family. Don't let it happen.

This brings up the question of what motivates you, as well. If you are tempted to go to a family member to ask for money, what is your purpose? Do you not trust your own ability to create your own funds? There are times that the economy can be tough, and we may need to ask for help when we may be short. But that is different.

Ellen's husband Danny was dying of kidney cancer when his sister Susan stood in for Ellen while Ellen ran an errand. They were standing vigil for Danny; he was bedridden and very weak, and didn't want to be left alone. In this case the result was a catastrophe. When Ellen got back to Danny's bedside, Susan was gone and Danny was furious.

"Don't you ever leave my sister alone with me again!" Danny fumed.

What Susan had done was launch into a long tirade with this weak, dying man about where his money was supposed to go. The sister assumed (inappropriately) that he had a great deal of cash, and she wanted a share of it. She took that opportunity to harangue her brother about what she felt she had coming. She argued for the other greedy family members who had apparently sent her on a mission. Danny was in no shape for this kind of assault and it exhausted him. He was already almost near death, and this behavior was unconscionable. Susan had no interest in the comfort and care of her dying brother. From then on Danny's family was banned from his bedside. This upset his family, but it was the only way to protect him from their onslaught. He was able to die quietly, with his loved ones holding him.

It is a sad fact that money can twist people into committing crimes that are well beyond the bounds of polite interaction. In this family, it set forth a pitched battle over a man's deathbed, and forever split the two families over nonexistent riches. Toxic WordFood was used to create terrible rifts that last to this day.

Is this a theme in your life? Is money, or the lack of it, making you into something or someone you don't like? This takes us back to the WordFood you feed yourself every day, and the simple faith you have in yourself and your ability to create your own abundance.

FOOD FOR FAITH

When you are brought into this amazing world, you are given the chance to experience life in all its many forms. How you embrace this journey is up to you. You draw your life experiences to you. There are no victims here. This is the huge responsibility in life, to realize that our lives are our own, to be lived on our own terms. We bring events toward us and we derive important lessons from them, if we are wise. When we cry "Victim!" we are missing the point.

You are never in any situation that you cannot handle. Quite the contrary, you are where you are precisely because you are ready to take on the challenge you are facing. It's up to you to have enough courage to step up. No one is playing puppet with you. No one is singling you out to make you suffer. That's your ego talking. You just aren't important enough to garner that kind of attention. Along with everyone else in the world, you have a job to do: wake up and take responsibility for your life, your emotions, your personal development, for the wake you leave in the lives you touch. When you have faith that you have considerable ability to create your own positive conditions in life, you create abundance. When you are committed to crying "Victim!" you will create scarcity. If by crying victim you get others to take care of you, that's a shallow kind of life. But it's not one of courage, of abundance, of living out loud. That's a decision for you to make.

What do you say to yourself in the mirror? What is the conversation you have running in your head every day with your precious self? Do you convince yourself that you should be pitied? Are you confusing pity with love? Do you get yourself going by telling stories about getting even with someone? Is your morning ritual full of self-loathing or self-pity, fantasies of revenge for the world's wrongdoing?

YOU MAKE YOUR OWN WAY

There is a different life available to you right now that is free from all this anger, and that is to see the world as one that does not owe you anything. The world simply does not, and never did, owe you any more than the opportunity for you to create a life. No one else owes you anything, either. You make your own way. If anything, you owe others your courtesy, your genuineness, your honor and graciousness. What you put into life, you get back. That is what changes your experience in the world. When you live with gratitude for the opportunity to be alive and make a difference, to participate in this experience, life gives back a thousand fold. When you view the world with meanness, or through a scarcity mentality, convincing yourself that the world owes you a living, you will perceive that everyone is trying to get something from you, and you will perpetually live in a state of fear. You will have a stunted existence and you will feed yourself toxic WordFood every day making sure your worldview is correct. How will you choose to live?

The WordFood you feed yourself, the conversation you have running in your head all day, determines the quality of your experience throughout your life. When you change the quality of the diet you feed yourself, you change the quality of your life. Put on your plate servings of Heartbreads, Energy Enhancers, Character Fiber: verbal nutrition that builds up the relationship you have with yourself. Each day greet yourself with enthusiasm and love, the way you would a beloved child. This is the only true relationship you will ever have—and the one that deserves the most attention. The language you use with yourself determines the quality of your day, every day, all day long. Who's talking to you inside your head? Make sure that whoever is doing the talking has your best interests in mind, and is giving you messages of encouragement and love. Each time you catch your image in a mirror, send yourself a caring message.

If you find changing this internal conversation is too hard to do alone, get professional help. Sometimes this is the only way to redirect how we speak to ourselves. It's not an act of defeat to seek counseling; it's a brave step. What's important is that you've made a move toward a healthier life.

Personal growth is hard, challenging work. It is also the door that opens up to a different life, a different way of seeing and experiencing life through different eyes. When you start speaking kind and respectful WordFood to yourself every day, your experience of yourself will change. And from that, your experience of others will shift. It won't happen overnight, but it will evolve. You will see the world as more welcoming, people as more friendly. You will want to take part in the world more. And you will not see the world as a threatening place, or yourself as a victim in it any more. You will want to make a difference. WordFood spoken to yourself with love every day is transformative.

COACH!

In the process of writing this book I have been made far more aware of the importance of having authentic conversations. Recently I told my speaking coach that, twenty years ago, he intimidated me. This surprised him.

"Really?" he said, "I intimidated you?"

"I was embarrassed that you might find out that I wasn't the big shot speaker I wanted you to think I was," I explained. We both laughed, because this is why one hires a coach. But it has taken me twenty years to tell this man the truth, to hire him, to feed him the kind of WordFood that leads to our working together so well.

What keeps you from authentic conversations? Are you afraid of looking silly, stupid, ridiculous? Is it your pride, your ego, your inflated sense of self? Your fear of not looking cool? For twenty years I didn't hire coaches because I was embarrassed that they would find out that I wasn't already polished. That's like cleaning the house before the housekeeper gets there!

Today I work with four coaches and I am humbled regularly by the wisdom of each of them. That is why I work with them, because they are good at what they do. Their expertise makes me better, and they feed me excellent WordFood. They know when and how to push me and what kind of WordFood I need to hear to grow beyond my boundaries. That's what good coaches do.

My business coach keeps me in line about financial issues now that my sales skills are where I want them. She and I work together to make me an increasingly better businesswoman and she is always pushing me on my weak spots: detail orientation, finances, finances, finances! Since hiring her, my sales have increased substantially and so has my business knowledge.

My personal trainer keeps me in shape appropriate to my age and body type. He challenges me every week to push beyond my limits and find a new level of fitness. I'm in my best shape in years.

My spiritual coach works with me to keep me focused on my personal growth and my inner development. He is constantly challenging me to find answers to the big questions and to seek a different life, one full of love and service.

Finally my writing and speaking coach works with me regularly to hone my professional skills as a speaker, to perfect techniques of my craft, to be a better presenter and author. Since working with him I have seen significant growth in both these areas.

You may not wish to invest money in coaches. You can find free mentors in many situations instead. People get invested in you when you get them excited about your dreams—that's WordFood at work! Let them know what you want to accomplish and ask for help. You can make friends with someone at the gym and find a workout partner. At your place of worship you can ask for extra guidance with your inner development. The SBA has all kinds of business development and training programs for people with businesses—just for entrepreneurs. There are so many ways to get help from superiors at work who want to see you succeed as well. I simply choose to hire the help and have these talented people as my Board of Directors. It took me a long time to see how valuable they would be but now I'm a powerful believer. Get coached—however you can make it happen. We all need positive WordFood even if we can't get it from our families.

Some of your best coaches could well be your kids, who will forever be your best mirrors and truth tellers. If you ever need a good dose of reality, sit down for a conversation with your six year old. Or your 'tween. The truth might not be delivered in a graceful way, but it will be unfettered and probably funny, like a sucker punch.

Coaches are the sources of some of the most honest and authentic WordFood you will ever hear. In order for you to grow into what you are meant to be, your coaches will push you. The good ones will not listen to your excuses, your whining, your arguments, your toxic WordFood to yourself. They will, like my Drill Sergeant Green in Basic Training, get up in your face and call you on your bulls__t and make you do another twenty in the dirt. And when you cry, you do another twenty. And another. And then when at the end of all that blood, sweat and tears you turn in the finest performance of your career, your own personal Drill Sergeant Green will be the one whose piercing celebratory whistle will ring loudest above the applause.

Go find yourself a coach, who will feed you WordFood, the nectar of the gods, which will straighten your spine and fill you with mettle and remind you what you're capable of doing. Whether it's to finally write that book, get that big job, write the challenging resume or move up the corporate ladder, get the support you deserve. Remember, there isn't a single great athlete in the world that has gotten where he or she is without the help of many great coaches. Each of us needs help as well. No child is raised, no book is written, no building is built, no great project is completed wholly alone. We all need help, and the sooner we learn to ask for it the happier we all will be.

Our coaches, our mentors, become integrated into our lives in remarkable ways. They know us intimately: our weaknesses, our great strengths, our capacity for the best and the worst. They know what we need to achieve our dreams. And they can become our greatest allies because of this knowledge. Our coaches are some of the people with whom we can have our most authentic conversations about ourselves. That is why it is so essential to get a mentor, a coach, someone who is invested in your personal and professional development. These mirrors are the guides through the labyrinth of life. Along with the rest of our relationships, they will show us the truth of who we really are, and what we can be.

Ask for coaching inside your family, too. Offer it first to your loved ones who deserve this from you. Find ways to provide WordFood to your spouse, your kids, and your kin in ways they haven't experienced before from you. Give them the kind of help and loving sustenance that you'd like to get from them. Give first what you want to get. Show them how it feels. Find out what they're trying to achieve and help them get there. Then you can ask for their support. You might be surprised at who shows up for you once you've done this. It will lead to genuine, important WordFood that leads to real relationships.

In some cases you may really be on your own, with no fourth cousin thrice removed to call on. In this case you will need to start making up your own family as you go. I left home at sixteen, and as I traveled around Florida finishing up high school I met lots of people. I met families and "adopted" them. In the same way I adopted high school kids as family, and their families as my extended family. It became easy, just a matter of taking a real interest in people and wanting to know all about them. I was a bit of an anomaly, a high school kid who was self-sufficient, so people were curious. But people were warm, and liked a friendly kid, and so I always had a home to go to when I got lonely and needed television time or a family meal.

This ability to be comfortable with strangers held me in good stead as I joined the Army and started traveling the world. Everywhere I landed I was always adopting another family: an ancient landlady with a dubious past as a bar owner in Chicago, the family I met by mistake when I went to the wrong address about a rental. We were dear friends for thirty years until they moved and left no forwarding address. Their family of four boys was my landing zone in Orlando for several decades. All because of a mistaken address!

Every Christmas I trek back up to Spokane, Washington to spend the holiday with one of my friends from The Hubbel Group. Jill's extended family Christmas is one of those dream gatherings of people who know how to cook, eat and collide with good humor, enthusiasm, stories, kids, presents and general bonhomie. There are never any spats, walkouts or temper tantrums that otherwise tend to mar the holidays of many folks. For the last five years I've found myself at their table for the triad of Christmas events—Christmas Eve, Christmas breakfast and Christmas dinner at the various houses of family members, happily sharing presents and food and hilarity. They welcomed me once and after that I was family. Until I have a family of my own, this is where I am from December 21 to 28 every year. Jill has been and continues to be a mentor of mine starting from our Great Broad days and to this day she is the source of great WordFood, as I am for her and her endeavors. One of the rewards of that friendship is Christmas.

I believe we can fabricate our families where we are planted. We can create rich and loving relationships even if life did not grace us with storybook relatives. We can choose to feed ourselves toxic WordFood about the bum deal we got, or we can look around at the extraordinary people who surround us and make a pretty damn good family of our own. Nothing can diminish your capacity for love but your own fear of loving to the limit.

STUCK ON AUTOMATIC PILOT

I had a watershed conversation with an old friend recently in which we both revealed that we had harbored impressions about each other many years earlier that had kept us from having a much closer relationship. My impression of this man was that he was on a pedestal, a bit arrogant, a high achiever and that, in his eyes, I wouldn't amount to much more than a gnat. Contrary to my impressions, he had always had a high opinion of my skills and wanted to support my career and have a closer relationship. As the years have gone by, this man has softened his approach in the world, and I have gained a greater confidence in it, and harbor far fewer fears about how I look to others. This has created a space where a new kind of conversation can take place, and a new kind of friendship can happen.

This new conversation took place because I shared some caring HeartBreads. It got us talking about us, and then about how people can go their entire lives stuck in a rut without changing the nature of their relationships. Our discussion allowed us to enter new ground with each other and, as a result, a richer appreciation for each other.

What relationships in your life are on automatic pilot? Janet and Justine were friends for twenty years and found themselves in Paris together for fifteen days. They ended up in a major fight, having discovered differences and a long running disagreement between them that finally erupted in the forced intimacy of the trip. The two friends were committed to the relationship, and took the time and care to work out their issues. Not only did the vacation survive intact, more importantly, the two women came out of it much closer friends, having aired long-standing problems. Janet says that they moved to a whole new level of connection after Paris, finding a new language of connection.

How many of your relationships need an overhaul? How many people in your life may be feeling taken for granted? Do you feel taken for granted? Are you steaming about it? The other person involved may have no notion that you're feeling this way. They often don't. So often we can develop resentment because we imagine knowledge or feelings on the other person's part that have no basis in reality. The only way to know is to ask.

Janet said that with her friend Justine, it was a risk to get into the fight. Here they were in Paris on vacation. They were not only about to cut the vacation short, but risking cutting off a twenty-year friendship. Both might not survive, but the issues at hand had reached a point where they had to be discussed. It took courage on both their parts to move through their anger and their problems with each other. In this case, the relationship was rejuvenated. As Janet put it, "We cleared the air and were able to move on much closer to each other."

In every life there are connections that are on autopilot. Sometimes we are taking each other for granted. We get to the point where old familiar faces are just that: old and familiar. So much so that we stop recognizing their value to us. We aren't growing those associations. Those friends and family connections go stale and we stop feeding them and we get bored. It's up to us to inject something new into them and stop expecting them to do all the work to make us happy or feel entertained.

How can you challenge an existing relationship to be better? What needs to be said to clear the air? Ultimately the very things Janet feared saying to Justine were what saved their friendship.

Sometimes a blowup is what it takes to clean out the debris of a musty marriage or failing friendship. Longstanding anger can build up and sour an arrangement between people who otherwise love each other. They can choose not to talk about things because they fear hurting each other's feelings, but issues still remain and cause an undercurrent of resentment. These petty issues build walls, and over time the walls slow down the flow of attraction the way barnacles slow down a boat in the ocean. With that kind of buildup, it's hard to fall back in love, to rekindle the flame, to rebuild trust. There simply has to be kind WordFood that opens the door to a new way of speaking. Whether it starts with "I've been meaning to say this for a long time," or "I love you enough to finally say this out loud," it makes no difference. Someone needs to open the dam and it probably is going to be you. The other person may be totally unaware of your feelings, or may be aware and afraid of bringing up the topic.

AN OPEN HEART

The trick is to speak to each other from the heart, with plenty of servings of HeartBreads to protect the feelings of those we are addressing, and the Energy Enhancers as appropriate, but to check our intent going in. What are we there to accomplish? Are we there to do damage, get even, or set the record straight about being right? Then we need to clean house before we get started. Our WordFood can't come out free of clutter with those agendas.

You need to approach this with an open heart and a willingness to let things evolve wherever they go. You may find out you've been the bad guy in some ways and it may hurt. You may find out that something minor is going on. Anything can happen. But let go of the need to come out of this encounter on top, for that is not what WordFood is about. It's about keeping both of you whole.

When you go into this conversation, be open about what may or may not happen. Be grateful for any openness or willingness to discuss on their part. That's a good start. You may not get very far the first time. But with gentility, care and warmth, you can open the door to the first chamber, and then agree to come back again when things have cooled off. It is in how you handle the conversation and the person's dignity that you earn the right to come back and open the next door. You may find that the person you thought you knew so well is far more complex and, yes, interesting, than you ever knew. It is all about the how, and the HeartBreads and Energy Enhancers go a long way toward creating the environment to make this happen.

> *"I know this might be uncomfortable for you and you are very brave to do this with me."*

> *"I admire your courage to have this conversation with me."*

> *"This isn't easy for me either and I appreciate your willingness to talk."*

> *"You've always had a lot of guts and this takes more than usual."*

> *"I really appreciate your being here for me like this."*

> *"This means a lot to me that you would take this time to talk."*

"You're very important to me and that's why I want to have this conversation."

"This relationship means a lot to me. That's my priority that we work this out."

Whether it's a love affair, friendship, long-term marriage or a tiff that you're trying to keep from heading into a full-scale fight, loving WordFood is the key for reaching across the chasm between you to set the conversational "table." It sets forth how you intend to feed your partner and how you wish to be fed: with courtesy, regard and respect. You are setting the tone.

The truth is that such a conversation may end the relationship. If that happens, it was meant to end, and that is good news for you both, because you were hanging on to something that had ended a long time ago. As the legendary blues singer Muddy Waters once said, "You can't spend what you ain't got / You can't lose what you ain't never had."

In other cases, you will open up a discussion to a fresh start and a new way of being together. You may find some thorns that will prick along the way, but that's a small price to pay for greater intimacy. Many couples pride themselves on how "we never fight." If that is the case then they have no intimacy. People build closeness by moving through their disagreements and issues. Conflict ultimately builds trust. The ability to get through hard times is what teaches us how to treat each other, what kind of WordFood we wield when times get tough.

This is not a ticket to lay into your best friend about some complaint or petty argument. This isn't about complaining to your wife about taking care of the dishes. This is about handling long-standing, fundamental issues that lie at the heart of relationships, the kinds of things that eat at intimacy and slowly wear down on love or friendship over time. Like water on stone, when we can't trust each other in our closest connections, we wear down, and we are not being fed. And we need to talk it out, even when we fear the outcome. When you both are committed to the relationship, like Janet and Justine, the work that you do to get there will make you both stronger, and you will be secure in your relationship as a result. The conflict will strengthen you when you use respectful, kind WordFood to move through the issues.

When you unearth these kinds of issues, you may discover where one of you is being a jerk. The other is being rude on a regular basis. Someone is unkind. Or there was an incident years ago that went by without being handled for some reason. Anything could come up. What you must try to do is let these things surface without reacting to them. Don't be defensive. The purpose is to allow the hurts to rise and be heard so that they can be in the light of day for once. To defend is to put them back in hiding and defeats the purpose of this exchange. Use respectful WordFood:

> *"Thank you for that insight."*

> *"I appreciate your letting me see this part of you."*

> *"That's an important aspect of me I didn't see before."*

> *"I didn't understand that."*

> *"This is something to think about."*

> *"I can see you really care about this."*

Pushing back by blatantly stating the other person is wrong or doesn't understand will backfire. Accept what they say as valid from their viewpoint just as you would have them do for you. Try to keep your emotions in check. Honor that you both have investments in being right, but hear each other out. If you have set ground rules that you will use respectful WordFood from the beginning, this helps to keep the conversation clean of accusations, cursing, or other ugliness. When things get hot, this may be tough, but it helps to have an agreement up front.

You may find that the hurts you both have been nursing have no basis in reality. On the other hand, they may be well-founded, and need counseling to be worked out. But what has happened is that something that has been festering well below the surface has been aired out at last, and this relationship is well on its way to healing. You may find that simply the act of having the conversation re-kindles the interest between you because you had stopped talking.

Even if your conversational partner descends into accusations or anger, don't take the bait. Keep to the high standards that you have set with this WordFood and invite him back up to those standards. Acknowledge that you've heard him and understand his feelings and as best you can, try not to be drawn into an argument or de-fend yourself. The issues are on the table. Sometimes they don't loom so large, nor do they have the power they wield in our sub-conscious mind. We can address the fears we harbor, the grudges we've borne, and deal with them one by one with courage and re-spect until we've hit those that need external help or we've handled the list ourselves.

Be aware that you might discover that you've been committing microinequities for years. They don't just happen at work. They happen at home and in love affairs and in friendships. We can offend and hurt people at any time. In a marriage, husbands and wives can fling stinging barbs at each other every day for thirty years. Over time, they've built up such heavy layers of armor against each other's stings that they are no longer touching flesh. There is no intimacy in such a partnership.

ROLL UP YOUR SLEEVES

It takes courageous WordFood to begin a conversation about where we really are. Especially when there are kids involved, and property, businesses, belongings. Things. Another thing about my father is that he was a philanderer and my mother wanted out of the marriage. But my father refused. Not because he loved her but because they had a cottage on Chesapeake Bay with a lovely sailboat and a great many other amenities that would disappear without my mother's steel union salary. This was the late 1930s and things were very different for women back then. They stayed together, somehow produced two kids and remained in an unhappy, barbed wire union.

My parents had what my mother called "an armed truce," after years of throwing poison darts at each other. Theirs was a loveless, sexless marriage. They slept in separate beds at opposite ends of a long porch separated by a heavy green drape. They argued all the time, never touched and never hugged. They spent their time verbally crawling over each other, looking for vulnerable spots to dig in their barbs. This lasted fifty years until my father died of cancer.

Shortly afterward I flew my mother to California to spend time with their long-time widower friend Ed. He was a kind, loving man, who radiated good cheer and sweetness. I was standing on his porch with my mother when tall, handsome Ed opened his door. My mother fell tush-over-teakettle in love right then and there with the only man who was ever truly kind to her. Until the end of her life in 2001, Ed returned her friendship but not her undying love (to her great frustration). To Ed's credit, he called her every Friday night for the last seven years of her life, read her dirty limericks, and sent her to bed with a smile on her face. That is how she died at 91, early on a Saturday morning, Ed's voice in her ears.

There is another truth to keep in mind when you begin this Word-Food conversation. Your friend, spouse or family member may not honor the ground rules. They may not care about your feelings at all. They may not have the same investment in the relationship, and you are going to find out where they stand.

You may have every good intention of turning things around, but your spouse actually likes things right where they are. Remember, relationships are hard work, and what you want them to do is roll up their sleeves and do the work with you. Sweat a little, do some heavy lifting, take some responsibility. That may be asking too much. This is a fine time to find out whether they've got the commitment you're looking for to move forward in the relationship the way you want to move forward. If not, then that's your answer. What you do next is up to you.

They may say that it's all your fault. They may try to make you feel guilty or shameful when it has nothing to do with you. They may be master manipulators. Some people just show up as assholes. The world is full of people who have agendas, who aren't very nice, or who don't have your best interests at heart. There are criminals and sociopaths and truly evil people out there. I have one for a second cousin. He's a bad operator and he wrecked an entire family. Who knows who else he has ruined? You may well have married or befriended one of them. This is great information for you—time to clean house and move on. And it's time to take a look at the choices you make for companionship.

CHANGING PEOPLE

You've heard this before. You can't change people. People have to want to change themselves. You can set an example, and people may or may not follow that example. But you can't force change. I have a friend who has been making changes in her diet and exercise program for years. She's hoping that her husband will be motivated to change his lifestyle, get out of his easy chair and do something about his thirty-pound weight gain and high blood pressure. All the exercise equipment they bought for him to use, she is using. She's lost forty pounds and is in excellent shape. Her husband, by contrast, can't walk two blocks without doubling over with back pain. They are in their late fifties and she is beginning to truly worry for his long-term health. When he is scared enough, or fat enough, he will start making changes. No cajoling, hounding, pushing, negotiating, or handing him articles about high blood pressure will make any impact.

The same thing goes for any aspect of how we interact with each other. My husband developed a drinking problem that escalated into alcoholism, which he strenuously denied. The march of large wine and liquor bottles to the curb on trash day, along with the occasional hole punched in the dry wall, were enough proof for me. Attempts to discuss this were met with argument and denial. Ultimately, during an ugly drunken brawl, I taped him. When I played back the recording of his rant, he was mortified, and I wanted out. I'd had enough of his verbal abuse. Within a few weeks he wanted to drink again. I asked for a divorce. There was no change coming.

This isn't to say I didn't add my own set of problems to the marriage, because I did, but this is what ended my commitment to making it work. I had hoped he would change. I had hoped that the relationship was more important than the alcohol but I was wrong. So I made the choice for him.

I lived with my husband's alcohol consumption until the night his office called and said he had fallen into the local lake during a party and he needed dry clothes. I brought them to the restaurant where they were having a dinner. On the way home, he lit into me. I happened to have a tape recorder between the seats, and I turned it on. For an hour, he called me every name in the book. He used every epithet he could think of. He accused me of things I would never even think of doing. He went to a very dark place. On the way home I heard the sound of my heart break and the fabric of my marriage ripping. I screamed at him for the first time in my life, a sound so full of despair I could hardly bear my own voice. I realized once and for all the hopelessness of our situation, when he stepped into the realm of verbal abuse, where I could no longer trust him. For me, that was the tipping point.

Sometimes you can't move forward, and you have to let someone go. There are things in each of us that we cannot change. There are aspects of our personality that are who we are, fundamental to our way of being. We can work on other things, like bad habits. When you have your conversation, you have to decide what can be worked with and what is non-negotiable. You may be surprised at which is which.

SEA CHANGES

My husband and I never talked about how we had started sitting at opposite ends of the couch, with the dogs between us. The dogs got all the affection. It just evolved that way, and it never came up. We should have talked about it. It was an early symptom of a marriage that was in trouble, and that ended not long afterwards. I had issues but instead of bringing them up, I just moved away from him physically. I was afraid of his anger, and he was angry that I was afraid of his anger. It was an ugly cycle.

When the dogs, or the cat, or the kids get all the love in your family, and your husband or wife is losing out, that's feedback. It's time to talk to your spouse about what's really going on. You may not even know yourself, but it's the beginning of the end when you stop touching. They do notice, even if you aren't paying attention. And it hurts them.

Many people choose to do nothing because they are physically comfortable in life and splitting up is just too messy and much too much trouble. Or it might bring up some pretty unpleasant topics and we just don't want to go there. That's why it takes courage to speak the truth and have authentic conversations. It does bring up the facts, and the facts sometimes cause our lives to take unexpected turns.

Those unexpected turns can be pretty fantastic. A longstanding relationship that has stalled can set two people free to find adventure. Two friends who have been secretly resentful of each other can find better company instead of harboring ill will. A fiftyish couple who "stayed together for the kids" can finally go off and find true love. Love and friendship don't have "use by" dates. People hook up and befriend each other all the time all over the world. WordFood is the key to starting those connections—to revamping the stalled ones—and to ending the bad ones gracefully.

People resist change, often strenuously. We find ways to avoid it, especially if it means uprooting our lives. But in many cases this very uprooting is what opens up the possibility of life happening to us. The chance to meet new people. The opportunity to make ourselves over at any point in our lives. Possibly to move to another part of the country or the world, even. To take up a new hobby or sport, get a makeover, learn a new skill, redefine ourselves. A positive WordFood conversation can lead to all kinds of things. The truth can do all this if you are willing to let yourself speak candidly with those you love. Let go of those relationships that do not feed you what you need. Rebuild at the heart level those precious relationships that deserve your attention and that need repair. And invite out of your life those toxic relationships that are draining away your energy, your time and your very being.

Where could there be more love, more fireworks, a closer connection, more fun? Where can a relationship deepen by sharing a revelation? This has to come from you. If you wait, it will never come. Like the Kevin Costner movie, *Field of Dreams*, if you build an open heart, that's only the first step. You have to create a magical opening night ceremony for every single special person in your life, and then they might come. For they have to open their hearts as well. Not everyone is willing to do that. WordFood will help set the stage, and there are lots of examples in this book that can help. The revelation is yours and yours alone, and it comes from the most honest part of you. The other person will know its truth right away.

Or maybe they won't. You may take a chance with your open heart and they just don't get it. Or they think you're trying to pull one over. They can be suspicious of your motives and come out swinging. They might say, "This is just one of your tricks." All the kindest, most loving WordFood in the world isn't working. They look at you as though you have a stalk of celery growing out of your forehead when you try a caring approach. Clearly, this isn't working. What can you do?

I have a family member for whom no amount of love will work. No entreaties, no loving words, no physical expressions of affection, nothing is welcomed. She is an anarchist and hates everyone. Her only wish is to be left alone. She feels the world owes her a living and always has. She hates to work and has always found ways to get men to support her, and then she sucks the life out of them and discards them. The one child we know she has had is lost to the rest of the family. There may be other children she has borne who have also been left to their fathers. A husband trying to reach this woman would be hard pressed making any progress. To this man I would say, "Run as fast as you can!" No counselor can help her. There are people who make their way through life like human wrecking balls and she is one of them. The older she has gotten, the more isolated she has become.

Sometimes we love these people because we're supposed to, we're expected to, because they're family. But when they are relationships of our choosing, there is no excuse to think we can save someone from themselves.

DETERMINED TO SELF-DESTRUCT

One of my closest friends nearly lost everything by thinking he could save someone. Some years ago my dear friend Peter found himself in a relationship with a stripper who had an eating disorder, was bipolar and an alcoholic. For some reason, he decided that he wanted to help her get well, and he stuck it out with her, month after month, despite her mood swings, drinking binges and the terrible fights. Pete has his own problems with alcohol, and a couple of old DUIs on his record that he needed to be careful about, but he felt that he had the situation under control. But, against his better judgment, he and Serena would still go out and have fun drinking. One night they were out having beers and had a terrific argument while driving home. Peter began driving too fast and a bit erratic and he got pulled over. His anger spilled over and had some words with the cops. Serena was no help, being loud and drunk herself. The cop checked Pete's record, and the result was disastrous. Ultimately he did six months in jail, lost his license and a dream job. Needless to say, he broke it off with Serena.

Today, Peter is clean and sober and has been for nearly three years. He's in a healthy relationship and earned his way back into his dream job. He's one of the lucky ones. What he finally realized is that you can't take a sick puppy that doesn't want to be cured and try to make it better. He got his own life on track, and then found someone who better matched his lifestyle.

If you're in a relationship where you're trying to fix someone, Word-Food isn't going to fix them for you. You're the one who needs fixing. You need love from you. And no one else can do that for you. It goes back to where we started this book: with the person you see in the mirror every day. When you find yourself in relationships where you're on constant cleanup patrol, picking up a drunk girlfriend or a boyfriend on crack who always needs money from you, get out now. You're the one who needs help and fast. Your choice of partner is a statement about what you feel you deserve, and how little you regard yourself. Don't tolerate this in your life. Find professional help from some quarter to help you get to a better place right now.

Too often, people allow themselves to be abused far beyond what happened to me. Situations quietly get worse and worse, yet we tolerate them for reasons only we can fathom. Our friends see what we are putting up with and tear out their hair. We believe Billy or Sally will eventually come around. They won't. Not for you, not for anybody, will they change, except in the most extraordinary circumstances. It's best for you to pick up stakes and move on, and ignore their pleas of "Baby, I promise to do better!"

But before you run off to another Billy or Sally, it's time for you to do some serious soul searching as to what makes you choose such relationship partners in the first place? Back to the mirror. Your Master Architect wouldn't have you set up shop with some-one who constantly hurt you, so why are you doing just that? If you can't find the answer, find a guide who can help you find that answer before you get into another relationship. Past performance is an excellent indicator of future performance. Clean house before moving in another tenant. Learn how to speak loving WordFood to yourself, and get loving WordFood from others in your life.

AND FINALLY . . .

Who is your authentic voice? Who is the real you? Which part of you is spinning stories to impress people and which part of you is speaking the absolute truth from the heart? Only you know the difference. And that is why you need to develop that hyperawareness of who is talking at any given time. WordFood is authentic and spoken from the heart. It is our truth—servings of healthy words provided to people in our lives so that they receive our best every day, starting with ourselves. If we are speaking to ourselves authentically, then we aren't fooling ourselves with victim stories and lies about our being less or more than anyone else. We know we belong here and can make a difference. We know we have work to do on this earth, and that we deserve a chance to do it. We need to be heard, and those who love us need to know our love for them.

WORDFOOD I SHOULD HAVE SAID . . .

If you don't want to be one of those sad people who are full of regrets at life's end and who aches over having not said or done the important things in life, it's hardly too late. There is plenty of technology available. From sending a tweet to renting a biplane to fly a sign across the sky, you can trumpet what you feel about people to the heavens right now, publicly or privately. You can call, write, email, tweet, voicemail, ping, leave a note on the fridge. You can choose your method of communication. There is no excuse for not letting the people in your life know right now, today, how you feel about them. Whether they live another fifty years or not you will always be glad you told them you cared, apologized for something dumb, took care of unfinished business, or handled an old problem. It may take some courage but the real win goes to you who took the first step toward healing the relationship.

There is magic in that move and in healing the human family. When you speak the WordFood of love, forgiveness and acceptance, it opens the heart for the world to start turning again inside you.

WordFood Extra:

"The Rule"

It's so important to establish boundaries. Here's a good related story. My friend and coach Orvel Ray Wilson and his wife Denise have what they call "The Rule," which has served them well through thirty years of marriage. "The Rule" simply states that, "No matter what else is going on, you have to be nice to me." And of course, it's reciprocal. Both agree to be bound by its simple, straightforward terms. That means that if either of them is in a foul mood, throwing a temper tantrum, having a bad day, they must still be kind to one another. No matter how frustrated, disappointed or angry they may be, they still have to treat each other with kindness and respect.

Orvel Ray says that, on more than one occasion, The Rule has probably saved his marriage. Both of them have personal issues that date back well into childhood, unconscious behavioral habits of scolding, rudeness or abusiveness that grate or cause hurt to the other. But The Rule is quickly called into play when this behavior raises its ugly head, and it usually works.

When Denise begins to scold Orvel Ray about leaving his dirty clothes lying around in the bedroom, Orvel Ray invokes The Rule.

> *"We agreed that you have to be nice to me. Even if I am a slob and I make a big mess, you still have to be nice to me."*

> *"All right. Will you please pick up your clothes and put them in the laundry."*

"Of course, darling. I'd be delighted to. I came in late and didn't want to disturb you. Sorry for the mess."

What's magical about The Rule is that it changes the tone of the conversation so that Orvel Ray isn't being scolded for leaving out his dirty laundry—he is, after all, an adult in his fifties. He may have simply been very tired the night before and forgotten. This way Denise is simply being asked to remind him nicely to take care of the chore, not nag him. And the same works if Orvel Ray imposes an ugly tone with Denise—she calls in The Rule with him.

The Rule ensures that these two people, who agreed to love and cherish each other for the rest of their lives, use loving WordFood in their everyday interactions. It is a gentle and fine reminder to come back to a loving exchange between partners who live and work in the same house. It acts as a safety valve, taking the heat out of the conversation before it escalates.

Some version of The Rule belongs in every relationship as a way to keep the partners conscious of their communications and to bring them back to why they connected in the first place. It is all too easy to live out our parents' relationships in our marriages, go unconscious and forget who we are. An agreement such as The Rule is a critical wakeup call that brings us back to the present moment with the partner we came here to love and respect.

If you recall, we said earlier that you cannot give this kind of gift without having it affect you. So each gift of kindness touches you as well, and transforms you in the giving. Every time you add value to another's life, you add value to your own.

The message throughout this book is that it all starts with you and your relationship with yourself. How you treat yourself and the WordFood you feed yourself every single day. There is no other relationship more important than this. Everything else in your life springs from this essential connection: how you treat you.

However, none of this means anything if you are not willing to temper your thoughts about yourself, and bring your own anger and frustration about your faults, your failures, real or imagined, to heel. You are the only one who can wipe the slate clean every single day of whatever wrongs you believe you may have committed. You and only you can forgive yourself of wrongdoings that most others have not noticed, but for which you hold grievances against yourself. Learn to let them go every day. You and your various parts will do things that are less than gallant or gracious every so often. That is being human. Ask others—and yourself—for forgiveness and move on. Let life be life.

Start each day with the knowledge that everything is new and there is much that can be accomplished with heaping servings of nourishing WordFood. This you can control.

When you face yourself, do so with the enthusiasm of someone who knows that this new day holds hope and promise and no guarantees but that you can control what you say, and you can put good WordFood into the world. That WordFood can touch hearts, improve lives, change perspectives, make people feel good and leave them feeling uplifted. And that is a great accomplishment for any human being.

To You, Gracious Reader

Thank you for taking the time to read this book. I genuinely hope you realize the power you have to change lives with your words. I wish for you to be the recipient of gracious and loving WordFood just as I hope that you will bequeath the best of all WordFood on everyone you meet.

I also want to hear your words. Please visit my website and blog at www.WordFood.com and let me know your thoughts.

About the Author

Julia Hubbel is an award-winning entrepreneur, international professional speaker, seminar leader and prize-winning journalist specializing in the art of communications and charisma.

Julia is a disabled, decorated Vietnam Era veteran who served as a journalist and television producer-director in the Army, and Chief of Military Protocol for the Jimmy Carter Presidential Inaugural in 1977.

In 1983 Julia hitchhiked solo around Australia, New Zealand and the Fiji Islands, learned how to fly ultralights and scuba dived the Great Barrier Reef. Her adventures have taken her to explore the great animal parks of Botswana, dive with Great White sharks and travel to other far-flung nations such as Thailand to learn languages and cultures. She has skydived 131 times and flown base on

a twelve-man star skydiving formation. She is a bodybuilder and cyclist, and an avid football fan.

In 1997, Julia created a diverse network of top-level professional women in the American Inland Northwest, using her model for establishing relationships. The Hubbel Group became a voice for professional women from all backgrounds and spun off companies, partnerships and lasting friendships. The remarkable story of The Hubbel Group is profiled in the bestselling book *Networking Magic* by authors Rick Frishman and Jill Lublin.

Julia has spent nearly three decades in senior corporate and consulting positions in the areas of training and organizational development in America, Australia and New Zealand. Her clients include Dell Computer, Southern California Edison, Archer Daniels Midland, Intel, Chevron, Hewlett Packard, Bank of America, Delphi, Cisco Systems, Qwest, Schering Plough, MassMutual, Sodexo, Lockheed Martin, Pfizer, and Microsoft.

Julia holds a Bachelor of Science Degree in Communications and Public Relations from American University in Washington, DC. She earned her certificate as a Supplier Diversity Professional in 2008.

WORDFOOD

Bring Julia To Speak To Your Group

KEYNOTES, SEMINARS AND EXTENDED WORKSHOPS TO HELP YOUR TEAM:

- *Improve employee morale*
- *Increase leadership skills*
- *Improve cooperation and teamwork*
- *Achieve greater intimacy and influence*
- *Avoid misunderstanding and arguments*
- *Strengthen bonds with coworkers, customers and clients*

To learn more about how WordFood training can benefit your group, call Brenda at 303 957 7149.

CPSIA information can be obtained at www.ICGtesting.com
Printed in the USA
266722BV00001B/5/P